BEYOND
BUSINESS
AS USUAL

BEYOND
BUSINESS
AS USUAL

VESTRY
LEADERSHIP
DEVELOPMENT

NEAL O. MICHELL

CHURCH PUBLISHING
an imprint of
Church Publishing Incorporated, New York

Library of Congress Cataloging-in-Publication Data

Michell, Neal O.
    Beyond business as usual : vestry leadership development / by Neal O. Michell.
      p. cm.
    ISBN 978-0-89869-569-4 (pbk.)
    1. Episcopal Church – Government. 2. Church management. I. Title.
BX5950.M53 2007
254′.0373 – dc22

                                         2007015823

Church Publishing Incorporated
445 Fifth Avenue
New York, NY 10016
www.churchpublishing.org

5 4 3 2 1

Contents

Part Two

EXERCISES FOR MOVING BEYOND BUSINESS AS USUAL

Acknowledgments

All of the vestries that I've worked with have contributed to this book, from the Church of the Redeemer in Houston, Texas, beginning in 1981, where I served on the vestry as a layman all the way to the vestry at St. Nicholas Church in Flower Mound, Texas, in 2007, where I currently serve as interim rector. This book was birthed out of our common life together. They have all taught me so much.

At Redeemer, Houston, I learned the value of an informed vestry. From St. Timothy's, Cotulla, I learned the importance of knowing the dynamics of the family relationships in the church. At Holy Trinity, Carrizo Springs, Texas, I learned the importance of developing leaders. While I served St. Barnabas, Fredericksburg, I learned how to become a rector and a leader of a congregation and how the past can be a catalyst for the future. At Redeemer in Germantown, Tennessee, I learned that there is a great difference between theory and practice and that community is a gift from God. As I served St. John's, New Braunfels, Texas, I learned the importance of trust being earned and that it doesn't simply go with the job title. In my time on the staff of the Diocese of Dallas, I began to articulate the things I had been learning in a way that seemed to be of value to others. Thanks go especially to the various lay and clergy leaders in the Diocese of Dallas that I have been privileged to work with. The quality of both lay and clergy leaders in this diocese would be the envy of any diocese. Working with them has been an honor and a gift. As the interim dean of St. Matthew's Cathedral in Dallas, I learned how the power of a church's history can give courage and determination to a church in transition. Finally, at Nick's in Flower Mound, Texas, I learned the balance between being a non-anxious presence and building a healthy urgency.

Great thanks and appreciation go to Cynthia Shattuck, my editor at Church Publishing, who came in the middle of the project and guided me through with a minimum of bumps and bruises. Thanks also go to Tom and Brownie Watkins for their hospitality in the use of their cabin at Sewanee to complete the majority of this manuscript and the Rev. Clay Lein for keeping me focused on mission.

Introduction

Our church was only a year-and-a-half old. We had grown consistently since our inception. Now was the time to hire a full-time Christian education staff person. Funding this position was a financial stretch for our young church, but everyone on our vestry was in favor — except for one member. He continually objected to and voted against this proposal because he "just couldn't understand why a church our size needs a full-time Christian education person."

I was stymied. I didn't know what to do. We made decisions by consensus, and we were at an impasse. I couldn't get this very committed lay leader to budge. I thought that I had earned everyone's confidence and that they would all consent just because I wanted to do it. I was wrong. We missed this opportunity, and the growth of the church was stalled as a result.

For two years we slogged through these vestry meetings until this person's term finally expired. I got to the point to where I dreaded these meetings. Although I blamed this recalcitrant member for my bad attitude, in truth, *I* was the reason for my bad attitude. I was not the leader that I thought I was. I had thought that since I was the pastor — and the one who had planted the church — that everyone would go along with any reasonable proposal I made. And, of course, in my estimation, every proposal that I made was reasonable.

The "One Thing"

To be truthful, I had actually spent several years as the pastor of the congregations that I had served being frustrated with the inconsistency of my leadership. Although two of the three previous churches that I had served grew under my stewardship, the growth of those congregations seemed, quite frankly, to be dependent on my own personality. I hadn't really made the connection between what

1

was happening in the church with what was happening among the vestry. Although the church grew, life on the vestry was "business as usual": Approval of the Minutes, Treasurer's Report, Old Business, New Business. I didn't know of any other way.

That changed when I hit upon the "one thing." What is the "one thing"? The idea of the "one thing" comes from the movie *City Slickers.* Mitch, the city slicker, played by Billy Crystal, has gone on a trail ride to get away from the pressures of the city and to "find himself." He encounters Curly, the trail boss guide played by Jack Palance, who seems fairly self-contained and content. Here's the dialogue from *City Slickers:*

CURLY: You know what the secret of life is?

MITCH: No, what?

CURLY: This. (Curly holds up one finger.)

MITCH: Your finger?

CURLY: One thing. Just one thing. You stick to that and everything else don't mean s**t.

MITCH: That's great, but what's the one thing?

CURLY: That's what you've got to figure out.

Translated into the world of business and church administration, I would say that I discovered the "one thing" that made a difference in the way I led the vestry. This "one thing" is what management consultant Marcus Buckingham calls the "controlling insight." The controlling insight that changed my way of leading vestries came from Peter Senge's book, *The Fifth Discipline: The Art and Practice of the Learning Organization.*

My Controlling Insight

I had been an attorney before attending seminary. To keep up my law license, I was required to complete a certain number of hours of continuing education each year. These continuing education courses were taught by some of the most successful lawyers, who were at the top of their practice and up-to-date on the latest cases in their particular area of expertise. Far from being bored and attending the courses simply because they were required, I always paid attention and even took notes. They were eminently practical.

As a clergyman I continued this practice, focusing on developing the skills that would help me to be a more effective pastor. Just as law school taught me to think like a lawyer but didn't teach me how to get to the courthouse, seminary taught me to think theologically but did not give me the skills to lead a congregation. I learned these from on-the-job training, what mentors I could find, and continuing education.

As I attended these continuing education events, I would return to the parish and continue my work having *absorbed* what I learned. But I never really discussed with my leaders what I was learning. When I read *The Fifth Discipline,* a light bulb turned on in my head. I came to realize that although I had been learning, I was not allowing the leaders of my church the benefit of learning along with me.

Senge says that a learning organization is where "people continually expand their capacity to create the results they truly desire, where new and expansive patterns of thinking are nurtured, where collective aspiration is set free, and where people are continually learning how to learn together."

What I have come to realize is that where the pastor of the congregation is in a continual attitude of learning, where he or she forms the vestry also to be learning continually, the result is that this attitude will spread throughout the congregation, resulting in a congregation that is willing to learn and more willing to accept changes, risk, and consequent failures along with the possibilities of greater successes. As I was perceived by members of the vestry as both knowledgeable and transparently still learning, they were free to mirror both my being knowledgeable and being willing to learn.

In seminary I had been trained under the "business as usual" approach. I am convinced that most of my seminary-trained colleagues were trained under this approach as well. If as priests, we just did tasteful liturgy, preached and taught with good theology, and provided decent pastoral care, the church would be just fine. We were trained for ministry in the 1950s. In the 1980s, this mind-set produced maintenance as usual.

This book is for those churches that are no longer content with business as usual. It is for those clergy and vestry members who want to be partners in ministry and mission as they explore new and creative ways to do and expand mission and ministry.

How to Use This Book

Most resources for clergy and vestries deal only with the business end of things, what the denominational and diocesan canons and local by-laws require, how to conduct a meeting, and so on. This is really a book on vestry leadership formation. The premise is that the rector or vicar (the pastor) has the primary responsibility and privilege as teacher to help form his or her vestry into a learning community. This book was written out of both my failures and successes in leading vestries as a parish priest. I pray that this book will help you and your vestry avoid some of my mistakes and become effective in leading churches to expand the reign of God in our communities. The aim of this book is to help pastors and vestries to develop their churches as learning communities.

The underlying premise of this book is that just as formation is important for the life of the individual Christian, so is formation important for the collective life of vestries. Simply stated, it is asking clergy and vestry members to change from simply taking care of the business affairs of the congregation to becoming missional in their orientation. The path to being a missional congregation runs through becoming a learning community.

This is also a book of resources to help form you and your vestry as a learning community. It deals with the "soft" side of leadership. More than a "how-to" book on vestry leadership, it is a book that, I hope, will enable the pastor and vestry together to journey along the leadership path. The first part of this book is an extended argument aimed at convincing you that the vestry as a learning community is the most effective model for leadership. Each chapter has one or more questions for individual or group reflection.

The second part is a series of lessons and interactive learning and discussion to be used with the vestry to help form them as a learning community. There are four different kinds of learning resources: Bible Studies, Teachings, Mental Exercises, and Reflective Readings. Different people have different learning styles, and some may prefer one style of learning over another. Be sure to read the introduction to this section for suggestions on how to use these materials effectively.

Discerning the right learning path for you and your vestry is where the art of leadership comes in. So, before you dig into the resources, be sure to read chapter 5, "Discerning Your Vestry's Pinch Points." As you reflect on where the pinch points are in your vestry, select those chapters or those learning resources that will speak to them. An introduction to the resource materials also suggests which resources might be used for the various issues confronting you and your vestry and the best path to follow in your own formation.

Part One

A New Way for
Clergy and Vestries to Think

One

Defining Reality

Our Churches Are in Decline

"Houston, we've had a problem."
— Astronaut Jack Swigert, Apollo 13

Parish ministry these days is increasingly complex and dynamic. That is because our society is increasingly complex and dynamic. The conditions today in which church leaders operate are much more demanding than they were fifty years ago, and they require a different approach to parish leadership.

Cultural Changes

In the late 1950s Americans began to be concerned about culture shock. In 1970, Alvin Toffler popularized and made readers aware of the phenomenon of "Future Shock," which is the challenge for people to cope with the unprecedented changes brought about by the new technologies. We now hear about the problem of information overload. With e-mail, twenty-four-hour news, and bloggers, we see the battle being waged between "old media" and "new media." A recurring question is: who is in control of the flow of information? The answer is: no one. Now anyone with a computer and access to the Internet can be a news reporter and have the world as an audience.

Suffice it to say, much changed between 1960 and the year 2000. This is true in all areas of politics, government, and education as well as everyday life. Similarly, running a business has become much more complex, with added requirements, warnings, safeguards, methods of operations, permits, reports to be filed, and government regulations to be satisfied.

This increased complexity affects the local church as well. In 1960, a church with an average Sunday attendance of 250 could function quite ably with a full-time priest, a volunteer Christian education staff person, a part-time secretary, a part-time organist/choir director, and a part-time sexton. Today that same church will likely have two full-time ordained persons, a full-time secretary, and a full- or part-time administrator, Christian education coordinator, organist/ choir director, youth minister, and possibly a new member evangelism coordinator.

Additionally, the increase in numbers of denominations and non-denominationally affiliated church networks has added greater complexity. Denominational distinctions are more blurred now, with Baptist and Presbyterian churches celebrating Holy Week, Methodist churches offering "Anglican style worship," and Episcopal churches having praise bands and projecting words for music and liturgy on overhead screens. Further, the ecumenical movement has made it easier and more common for people to shift from one denomination (or non-denominational church) to another.

As a result of the changes in our culture and the proliferation of worship styles and choices as well as the blurring of denominational identity and the general information overload that many people experience, it is difficult for the average church to set itself apart from other churches in the area. Churches must do more than tasteful liturgy, good theology, and decent pastoral care in order to minister effectively in the twenty-first century. Your parishioners can turn on the television and hear really excellent preaching. While the average Episcopal priest may not agree with the theology informing the preaching, there is no arguing that these televangelists are compelling preachers. This excellent, easily accessible preaching has put even greater pressure on all local churches.

Decline in the Episcopal Church

A review of the membership numbers of the Episcopal Church since 1965 reveals that, except for a few years in the late 1990s, the Episcopal Church is a denomination continually decreasing in membership.

The year 1965 was the high-water mark for baptized members in the Episcopal Church. From 1965 to 2003 our denomination lost nearly a third of its membership. Further, the average size of our churches has declined as well. In 1960, the average Episcopal church reported 450 baptized members. In 1965, the year of our highest membership, the average was 480 members per church. The average membership in our churches has declined to 32 percent (310 members per church) in 2005.

Although specific statistics have attempted to draw conclusions about the growth and decline of churches according to size, these studies are inconclusive. My own observations from studying Episcopal churches over the past fifteen years is that while some of our very large churches have gotten even larger, a greater number of middle-sized churches have decreased in size, resulting in more of our churches having fewer members than in years past. In 2002, 60 percent of Episcopal churches had an average Sunday attendance of 100 or less; in 2003 61 percent of Episcopal churches had an average Sunday attendance of 100 or less; and in 2004, this number increased to 62 percent. Similarly, the median average Sunday attendance in 2002 was 79, in 2003 it was 77, and in 2004 the median attendance was 75. Can you feel the creeping decline?

In short, many, if not most, of our churches have not responded well to the changes that have occurred in American culture since 1965. The result is that we have fewer churches than we did in 1965, and those church that we do have are generally smaller than they were in 1965. Today, the typical Episcopal church is basically a single-cell, non-complex organization in an increasingly complex culture. Consequently, this means that being a lay leader in the church, such as serving on the vestry, is an ever-increasing challenge.

A Word about Church Growth

Church growth has gotten a bad reputation in many parts of the church today. Many of the criticisms aimed at the church growth movement are justified when focusing on church growth minimizes the call to make disciples. We are called to make disciples and not simply to gather a crowd. I like to talk more about congregational development than church growth, because our aim should be to form faithful communities of disciples rather than just getting more people to church.

However, as the saying goes, "Please don't shoot the messenger." Our dislike or discomfort with the idea of church growth should not make us complacent concerning the decline in membership in our churches. I have heard many people say that we shouldn't be so focused on numbers, that we leave those things up to God. However, each number represents a person for whom Jesus died. The Lord who left the ninety and nine for the one lost sheep would say that those are not numbers but individuals. Personally, I find it hard to believe that God is honored by an American denomination that has lost a third of its membership over the last forty years!

It is natural for healthy things to grow. This is true of both plants and people. Given a proper amount of soil, nutrients, water, and light, plants will do what comes naturally, that is, they will grow. If a plant does not grow as expected, we look for the reason why. The soil may be malnourished, or it may have the wrong mixture of nutrients. Or the plant may need more sunlight, or less; or more water, or less. Some plants cease to grow because they are root bound because the pot is too small. To discern why a plant isn't growing, look for an unseen obstacle that is hindering the growth of the plant.

The same is true of churches. Often our churches don't grow because there are unseen obstacles that have hindered the growth that is otherwise natural to the life of the church. If we, as leaders, can recognize those obstacles to growth and replace those obstacles with healthy practices, the church will grow naturally — with, of course, a life-giving gospel proclaimed and with prayer and the work of the Holy Spirit.

We start with the mission of the church. According to the catechism of the Book of Common Prayer, the mission of the church is "to restore all people to unity with God and each other in Christ." As the church is accomplishing that mission, one has to assume that individual expressions, i.e., churches, of the larger church will grow larger rather than smaller.

If our denomination is collectively in decline, it is because many of our churches are individually in decline. So how do we arrest this decline in our churches? Who is responsible for leading our churches to engage our culture with the gospel in such a way that more and more people, as former archbishop of Canterbury William Temple said, "may be led to believe in Jesus Christ as Savior, and follow Him as Lord with the fellowship of His Church"?

For Individual or Group Reflection

- *Is your church in decline, plateaued, or growing? Make a chart of your church's average Sunday attendance for the past ten years. Also, review the ministries that have been started or ended during the past ten years.*

- *If these trends continue, what can we predict about the future of your church?*

- *What are the strengths of your church? What has caused the greatest growth or decline in the past five years?*

Two

Who Is Responsible?

"Who's on first?"
— Bud Abbott to Lou Costello

There are a number of Episcopal churches that have experienced re-markable growth over the past forty years, but as our brief survey of statistics indicates, most of our churches that were in existence in 1965 are smaller in 2005 than they were in 1965. The Episcopal Church has been living with this decline for the last forty years, and at this time, things don't seem to be improving.

So who is responsible for arresting the decline in membership and attendance in our churches?

In a sense, everyone is responsible for the decline; but when every-one is deemed to be responsible, no one is ultimately held accountable. I believe that it is the local vicar or rector along with the vestry that can arrest this decline and spur our churches on to greater growth. Let me begin with a true story.

What Use Are Vestries?

In a town that I once served, there was a local Baptist church, which we'll call Hillside Baptist Church. At that time it was the largest Bap-tist church in town. It originated in a church conflict within the downtown church that resulted in a group of dissatisfied members splitting off from the mother church. The "split off" church really didn't do much in its first several years of existence. It was simply one more tiny church birthed out of a church fight.

One day they called a new pastor. Within several years, this church grew until it was larger than the mother church.

Being new to town and having heard this story, I scheduled lunch with this very effective pastor who had turned this church around. I asked him not to be shy but to tell me the reasons for the growth of his church.

He replied, "I'll tell you, Brother Neal. When I came to Hillside Church, they had a congregational meeting once a month to decide the affairs of the church. They were paralyzed by all the arguing and voting. So, I decided to quit calling these monthly congregational meetings. We became a staff-run church, and the church grew. Now the only time we meet for a congregational meeting is when we need to borrow money or buy real estate."

Hmmm. This church grew from an average Sunday attendance of seventy-five to over five hundred without a lay governing board? This pastor was not an obviously charismatic or dynamic person. His preaching skills were adequate but not exceptional. He was a good, solid pastor to his congregation, but he would probably not draw a crowd on the lecture circuit. So what can we learn from this?

One thing we can learn is that it is quite possible for churches to grow without vestries. I suspect that vestries more often impede growth than foster growth in the local congregation. If that is true, then what use are vestries?

Our canons require that our churches elect vestries to serve as the legal representatives on behalf of the congregation. Basically, we have to have them because they are required.

Are vestries, then, simply something we have to have, and we'll just have to cope with them as best we can?

I believe not. I believe we can do better. I believe that service on the church's vestry can be energizing for individual members and that vestries can play a significant role in the growth and effectiveness of the local congregation.

"Lead, Follow, or Get Out of the Way"

Although denominational policies and distribution of resources can do much to strengthen the local congregations, it is the local rector and vestry that can have the most influence on the growth or decline in our congregations. Given the forty-year decline in our congregations, our clergy and vestries do not have a very good track record. Thomas Paine, pamphleteer during the American Revolutionary War, first said, "Lead, follow, or get out of the way." As a person who has been attending vestry meetings for over twenty-five years as a lay person, parish priest, and now diocesan staff member, I have sat through innumerable maintenance-driven vestry meetings. Many vestries get bogged down in the smaller issues of administration and never really get to the greater issues of vision, mission, and policy.

It is possible to grow a strong church with a weak vestry. As the story of Hillside Baptist Church illustrates, some churches might grow if their vestries would simply get out of the way. But I believe that it is impossible to grow a strong church with a strong vestry that is at odds with the rector, and continuously tries to keep the rector under close reins, or tries to micromanage the affairs of the congregation.

By their nature, vestries are conservative. They were designed as a check and balance on clergy authority. When the clergy and vestry work in tandem with each other, the parish is able to move forward. When they are at odds, conflict ensues, and the parish suffers. There are four options available to vestries in their relationship to their congregations.

1. *They can gum up the works*. A vestry can challenge every new initiative, hold the reins on new spending in the name of fiscal responsibility and thus stymie the growth of the congregation.

2. *They can follow*. If they only follow, they deprive the congregation of their insights and good judgment.

3. *They can get out of the way*. This is more desirable than gumming up the works, but in so doing, they become irrelevant. These vestries will eventually grow frustrated with being irrelevant and will likely rise up in protest and overreact in ways that are not in the best interest of the congregation.

4. *They can lead*. They can only lead in cooperation with the rector. If they try to lead ahead of the rector, then the congregation gets confused. They can hear only one voice at a time.

How can we so form our vestries that they are able to fulfill their appropriate check and balance role while not getting bogged down in minutiae, nor functioning too adversarially, nor ending up as simply the rubber stamp for the rector's initiatives?

Here's another true story. The names have been changed to protect privacy.

"He Said That He'd Never Ever Serve on a Vestry Again"

In one parish I served we were approaching new vestry elections. I was relatively new to the parish at the time, and I believed the church needed some longtime members to serve on the vestry. One of those that I considered, Bill, was a retired doctor who had been a member of the church for over thirty-five years. As I vetted his name with a couple of our current leaders, I was told that Bill would never consent to run for the vestry. When he had served on the vestry previously, he said that all they did was argue, and he swore he'd never serve on a vestry again.

I was convinced that he was a person of real influence and trust in the parish whom the congregation needed to have serve at this time, but he had pulled back from leadership in the congregation because of the acrimony he had experienced during his previous vestry service.

Having prayed about it, I finally approached Bill and told him that I saw him as a person whom a large number of the congregation truly respected and trusted and that the church needed him to serve on the vestry at this crucial time. Despite his protestations, Bill finally consented to let his name be put forward, and he was elected to serve on the vestry.

So positive was his experience of serving on the vestry that he was appointed as senior warden for the next two years and would recruit new members for the vestry by telling them that this was the best vestry he had ever served on and how much he loved serving on the vestry now.

Ask yourself, have you ever known anyone that actually *enjoyed* attending vestry meetings and serving on the vestry?

There is a better way.

For Individual or Group Reflection

- *What is the most significant thing that your vestry did in the past year?*

- *What do you enjoy most about serving on the vestry?*

- *Have you ever had a really positive experience of serving on a vestry or a board of directors? What made it positive?*

Three

What Is Your Mental Model?

"In theory there is no difference between theory and practice. In practice there is."
— *Yogi Berra*

It is in the order of things in this world for things to fall apart, cool down, or burn out. Cars break down, buildings fall into disrepair, a hot pan cools off when taken off the stove. In physics this is illustrative of the Second Law of Thermodynamics, which says that in a closed system, energy gets dispersed, or that entropy increases. Systems increase in their disorder. When you have a pot of water on the stove, you have to keep the heat turned on to keep the water boiling. If you don't keep the heat turned up, that is, if you don't continue to pour new energy into the system, then the water cools down. In other words, energy gets dispersed and entropy increases.

This is true not only in the physical world but also in the world of human interaction as well. The dynamics of group life are such that when there is no real leadership in a group — no energy poured into the system — then groups tend to move to the lowest level of commonality. Conversations in a group setting usually gravitate to the lowest common denominator. The Second Law of Thermodynamics suggests that unless energy is poured into the group, what results is not greater order or effectiveness but greater disorder and ineffectiveness.

Most vestry guides deal pretty well with the business side of the role of a vestry, such as job descriptions, fiscal responsibility, and so on. Those are really the functional obligations of the vestry. However, knowing the canonically based duties of vestry service is a necessary beginning but does not provide nearly enough training for an effective vestry. Knowing the canonical requirements alone are no more than dry bones. The question to ask is: can these dry bones of the vestry live?

Using the analogy of entropy and the Second Law of Thermodynamics, what our churches and vestries need are ways to "pour more energy" into our systems. The purpose of this chapter is to show the importance of developing a mental model for the vestry and to describe some of the less effective mental models that some churches use, as well as the most appropriate mental model for the vestry.

First we need to say a few words about the role of the pastor and the importance of the pastoral teaching office.

The Teaching Role of the Pastor

Crucial in the development of an effective vestry is the role of the pastor. An oft-quoted truism in Episcopal Church governance is that the rector has the responsibility for the spiritual concerns of the church and the vestry is responsible for the physical concerns. The effect of this kind of seemingly neat division of labor actually hinders the mission and ministry of the local church.

First, this dualistic construct separates the spiritual from the secular and often makes godly and spiritual laypeople feel like second-class spiritual citizens. While it is true that spiritual concerns are, indeed, the primary work of the church and the administrative aspects of the church are in service to the spiritual work, our sacramental understanding of life does not really allow us to separate the sacred from the secular so neatly.

Second, this approach often leaves clergy disconnected from the management of the church with lay people who feel as though the clergy don't really care about the overall well-being of the church. I have heard clergy say to lay leaders, "Do whatever you want with the programs; just leave the worship services alone. They are my province." By "getting out of the way," these well-meaning clergy are actually abdicating their leadership role and developing frustrated leaders who really do want to share in the ministry of the church rather than be mere recipients of ministry.

Church members often react to this dichotomy in two different directions. Some will protest: "The church isn't a business; it is a ministry. We don't base ministry decisions on business criteria." The second reaction is: "We need to run this church like a business. If something doesn't show a profit around here, we've got to quit doing it."

The truth is somewhere in between: the church is in the business of doing ministry. Churches live in both worlds.

The pastor is the shepherd of the flock, "laboring together with [those the priest is called to serve]...to build up the family of God" (BCP, p. 532). However, the pastor does not do the work of ministry alone. The pastor's responsibility is "to prepare God's people for works of service, so that the body of Christ may be built up until we all reach unity in the faith and in the knowledge of the Son of God and become mature, attaining to the whole measure of the fullness of Christ" (Eph 4:12–13).

Choose Your Mental Model

Building an effective vestry starts with developing the right mental model. What is the leader's mental model of what a vestry should be?

A mental model represents a psychological representation that the mind uses to understand real and hypothetical situations. A mental model is a sort of small-scale reality that allows people to anticipate events in order to give guidance for planning or simply for understanding. It allows the person reflecting to turn the mirror inward to unearth insights within and bring them to the surface for purposeful scrutiny.

A classic example of how a mental model can influence our action comes from Joel Barker's business training video entitled *The Business of Paradigms*. In the video he asks the audience to think back to the 1950s and consider the phrase "Japanese technology." He notes that what people generally think of are the little Japanese finger torture devices made of reed, characterized as "cheap," "junk," and so on. Then, when he asks audiences what comes to mind when they think of Japanese technology in the 1980s, they use terms like "innovation," "quality," etc. He says that our mental model of Japanese technology has changed dramatically since 1950. A business person with a 1950s attitude who deals with the Japanese in the 1980s and even today will likely make some very bad decisions based upon false assumptions and be in for a rude awakening.

We have already encountered one mental model for the vestry, and that is of the division between the spiritual and the material concerns of the church. This mental model has fostered divisions and turf battles between the laity and clergy for years.

The dominant mental model for the vestry in many churches is the institutional model. In this model, the church is viewed in terms of laws, deliberations, and committees. Robert's *Rules of Order* is present at every meeting and governs the procedure of the vestry. This model understands the church in a top-down sort of way. The *Rules* protects the rights of the minority against the power of the majority, but in the end the majority rules, and the minority submits. It assumes that debate and the need for an orderly control of the debate lie at the heart of how the vestry conducts its business. Ultimately, it proves to be inappropriate and ineffective for a faith-based community. This adversarial approach is representative democracy at its best — and sometimes its worst.

Applying this mental model to a vestry, we see that although different vestries may function in different ways, they all derive from this institutional model of the vestry.

Here are some "variations on a theme" of the institutional model for the vestry at work:

- Rubber Stamp: *"We're here to do whatever the priest wants."*

- Finance Committee: *"We're here to balance the budget (control spending)."*

- Elected Representatives: *"We're here to represent the values and concerns of the people who elected us."*

- Board of Directors: *"We're here to govern the church and act as liaisons to the various ministries in the church."*

- Loyal Opposition: *"We're here to make sure the rector (vicar) doesn't do anything too crazy."*

Your mental model will both shape your vestry and how its members relate to each other and the pastoral leader as well as help you determine whether your vestry is effective or not.

The basic problem with the institutional model for the vestry is that it is simply not very effective in helping churches deal with the highly fluid and turbulent times in which we live. It casts the vestry primarily as a debating society whose primary concern is to keep spending under control and take care of the church facilities. It causes the vestry to make decisions rooted in competition rather than cooperation. This institutional model of the vestry has dominated the polity of Episcopal churches since their inception. The model is characterized by debating and voting; winners and losers; in-power and out-of-power. The institutional model breeds division both in the church and among the vestry as the majority gets its way and the minority is made to feel like losers.

We need to turn to a more biblical model for the vestry.

For Individual or Group Reflection

- *Make a list of the vestry members from the past five years. How many are still actively involved in your church? What is their current level of commitment?*

- *Closer Look: How would you rate the energy level of your vestry? Hardworking and energetic? Taking care of business? Maintaining the status quo? Lethargic?*

Four

Vestry as Learning Community

"Sad is that day for any man when he becomes absolutely satisfied with the life that he is living, the thoughts he is thinking and the deeds he is doing; until there ceases to be forever beating at the door of his soul a desire to do something larger which he seeks and knows he was meant and intended to do."

— *Phillips Brooks*

The institutional model has proven to be an ineffective model for the vestry. Mimicking corporate boards of directors, Episcopal Church vestries have often taken on many of the worst characteristics of corporate boards and few of their positive ones.

Vestry as a Community of Disciples

An alternative — and healthier and more biblical — model for the vestry is that of a Community of Disciples. This model comes from Acts 6:2, where the early church had its first major disagreement. Here the Greek widows were being neglected in the daily distribution of food because the church had grown so large that the apostles simply couldn't get around to everyone. The resolution to the conflict was accomplished when "the twelve called together the whole community of the disciples" (NRSV) to address the issue. Out of this gathering the conflict was resolved and the church remained in fellowship.

The vestry is a community with a special ministry, namely, to lead the church. And the vestry is a community with a very distinct purpose: to share with the rector or vicar of the congregation in overseeing the spiritual and material concerns of the congregation.

So, what kind of community should the vestry aim to be?

The vestry should form itself as a microcosm of the congregation that they believe God is calling them to become. What is the vision of the church? Members should be able to look at the vestry and see that vision lived out — in the way that its members relate to one another, go about their business, and care for one another.

More than just conducting business as usual, the vestry is the particular community within the church whose responsibility it is — with the pastor — to cast vision, to embody the vision, and to establish policies that will enable that vision to be realized among the congregation.

This is an incarnational view of the vestry. Look at the vestry and you will see a microcosm of the church's vision being lived out. If the vestry doesn't live out that vision, any articulation of the church's vision by the vestry rings hollow; it comes across as, "Do as I say but not as I do." Any request for sacrifice is met with suspicion or complacency.

The most effective model, then, for the congregation — and, consequently for the vestry — is the learning community. The vestry that is continually learning as it expands the mission of the church better serves the congregation. Choosing the vestry as a learning community for your mental model of what you want the vestry to be will change the way that vestry members interact among each other, with the rector or vicar, and with the congregation as well.

Benefits of a Learning Community

A vestry characterized as a learning community has several benefits for the church and vestry. It sends a message to the members that:

- We're about learning around here and not so much about criticizing — because we are *all* learning.

- We know that there is a better way of doing things, so mistakes are a normal part of the learning process and thus are easier to forgive.

- We're focusing on the larger picture and leaving the execution of the details to the appropriate people.

Followers take their cues from the leader. If the leader is continuously open to learning, the followers will be more responsive to learning from the leader. In addition, focusing on learning stresses the joy of discovery rather than the burden of micromanaging.

Modeling a Teachable Spirit

Being a learning community starts with the priest. The priest sets the tone for the vestry as well as the congregation. That is why it is important that the priest display a teachable spirit. A priest with a teachable spirit enables and encourages congregational members to have a teachable spirit as well.

People with a teachable spirit have several characteristics.

First, people with a teachable spirit are able to reflect on and articulate what they have learned. They are able to pass on what they have learned to others.

Second, people with a teachable spirit are comfortable with their own mistakes as well as those of others. They recognize that they aren't the expert who has to have everything figured out but are able to shift positions and plans with new knowledge.

Third, people with a teachable spirit learn from their mistakes and the mistakes of people around them. They understand that learning from a mistake or failure can be just as important as having succeeded.

Fourth, people with a teachable spirit recognize that there are often several ways to solve a problem. Because there is not only one solution, they and those around them are able to come up with creative solutions; they are not immobilized by fear of failure.

Fifth, people with a teachable spirit exhibit a passion for what they are doing. They display a joie de vivre in ways that are infectious to those around them.

When the leader models a teachable spirit, those around him or her are freed to be teachable as well. Interactions among members of the group are more relaxed and engaging, and learning becomes fun.

For Individual or Group Reflection

- *Who was your favorite teacher in school? Why?*

- *If you have served on a vestry for a year or more, what do you know now that you wish someone had told you at the beginning of your time on the vestry?*

Five

Discerning Your Vestry's Pinch Points

"The Country Parson doth often both publicly and privately instruct his Church Wardens what a great Charge lies upon them."
— *George Herbert*

My underlying belief is that growth is natural to churches. The gospel is about transforming lives through the resurrected life of Jesus Christ. Where lives are being transformed, growth will follow. Growth is the norm for individual spiritual lives, ministry groups, and churches.

Churches grow when they are healthy. If growth is not occurring, it is likely because an unhealthy component is limiting growth, which is otherwise natural.

When vestries are not effective, it is likely there is a pinch in the system somewhere that keeps the system from flowing smoothly. This is sometimes difficult to discern because these pinches are intangible in nature. The intuitive leader will recognize where the vestry is stuck and work on that area to make it healthier. When one area of the vestry's life becomes healthier, the whole improves.

When reflecting on the effectiveness of the local vestry, if there is a problem, you'll likely find the pinch point in one of these four areas: spiritual, relational, administrative, and commitment. Before delving into the four areas, see the diagram on the following page that shows how these areas of vestry life fit together.

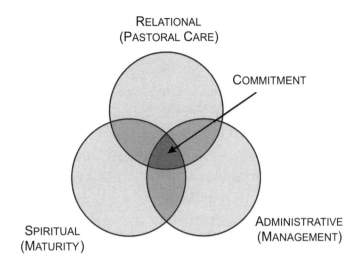

Spiritual Pinch Points

What is the spiritual level of your vestry? Is your vestry made up of immature Christians? Particularly if your group has a high visional motivation, vision among spiritually immature people can seem like a waste of time and cause the group to set its sights too low.

The spiritual level of the vestry will devolve to the lowest common spiritual denominator. Parishioners take their cues from vestry members. You can be sure that the church overall will rise no higher than the spiritual level of the vestry. The particular method of measurement used is less important than that the pastor actually has some means of measuring the spiritual level of the vestry.

Reflect on the members of your group. If not everyone in your group can be called upon to pray extemporaneously, you probably have a spiritual problem in your midst. Likewise, if you have members who are reluctant to share their spiritual journey, you likely have a spiritual maturity and intimacy problem. St. Paul told the Corinthians that they were spiritually immature — babes — and that he had given them milk and not solid food, because they were not ready for it (1 Cor 3:1–2). It's very difficult to engage in spiritual concerns when your group is made up of immature Christians.

Recall the various spiritual disciplines. Some can be exercised as a group. Most vestries will at least occasionally share the Eucharist together. Consider fasting together over a certain issue with which the vestry is struggling. This takes the decision out of the convincing arena and into the spiritual discernment area.

The wise rector or vicar or senior warden will take a serious spiritual assessment of the vestry and know what issues can be brought to the vestry. Time can be spent on individual discipleship in order to raise the spiritual level — and consequently the spiritual vision — of the vestry.

Relational Pinch Points

How are the relationships in your vestry? Is pastoral care needed among some members? Are there broken relationships? Is the time at the vestry meeting spent only in business? If two people are angry with each other and aren't reconciled, they will bring that enmity into the vestry meetings. Even if the anger or resentment doesn't come out in the group, it is a seed of discord that will keep the vestry from discerning effectively together as a group.

In small group ministry we talk about the number of "EGRs" in a group. EGR stands for Extra Grace Required. If you have too many needy people — generally two at any meeting — the group will focus on reacting or responding to the emotional needs of those EGRs. If the relationships are not generally healthy among the members, the group will not work cohesively together because these relationship issues are always lurking behind the scenes.

Time should be set aside periodically for the sharing of personal concerns and good news among individual vestry members as well as the congregation as a whole. Vestry members should be able to "rejoice with those who rejoice and weep with those who weep" (Rom 12:15, NRSV). Relationships are sustained by sharing and prayer.

Administrative Pinch Points

There may be an administrative clog in the system. Generally the smaller the church, the more communication is done via oral tradition. As a church grows in complexity, more intentional communications and administrative processes need to be put in place.

Attention should be paid to the church background of vestry members. Many times current vestry members will have served on a vestry at a previous church. If this church was either smaller or larger than the current church, they may be relating to the current vestry and making judgments and decisions based upon the size of their previous church. For example, if your church is a large program-sized church and a particular vestry member formerly served on the vestry of a pastoral-sized church, that member will often expect the larger church and vestry to function as a smaller pastoral-sized church and vestry, namely, in ways that are inappropriate and counterproductive to the current size.

Similarly, if group members were not given adequate orientation when they joined the group, they may not understand the ground rules for effective group membership or participation. Sometimes vestry members may have a difficult time making a decision because they haven't been given enough information or enough time to reflect and pray about a decision, or they don't have a sense of the group direction. What may come across as reluctance or being obstreperous might simply be a manifestation of an administrative pinch that can be remedied by some hands-on training.

Don't try to solve a spiritual problem with an administrative solution. Similarly, don't try to solve an administrative problem with a spiritual solution. Match the problem to the appropriate solution.

Underlying the spiritual, relational, and administrative areas is the important area of commitment. A church can have extremely capable and qualified members who relate well to each other, but if there are members who are lacking in commitment, the whole vestry and, consequently, the church, will suffer. Chapter 6 will explore the importance of commitment in the life of a vestry and its impact on the congregation.

For Individual or Group Reflection

◆ *How would you rate the spiritual level of your vestry? What are its strengths and weaknesses? What is the relationship between the spiritual maturity of the vestry and the work that it does?*

◆ *How long do your vestry meetings typically last? What does your vestry spend the most time discussing?*

— Six —

Commitment
The Glue That Binds the Vestry Together

"Those who make dissensions and disturbances in the church are the ones who seem to be what they are not." — *Augustine*

The relational, spiritual, and administrative areas of the life of the vestry mean little if the vestry members are not committed. Commitment is the glue that binds the vestry together. When a vestry member is lacking in commitment, that person becomes an EGR (Extra Grace Required person) in the vestry, and time and energy must be spent in "bringing that person up to speed" and accommodating his or her out-of-sync concerns.

There are three ways in which the commitment of the vestry member must be lived out: commitment to the local church and its activities, commitment to the vestry as a faithful and engaged member of the vestry, and commitment to the church in terms of contributing financially to the church commensurately with one's ability. Let's look at the importance of commitment for the effective vestry.

Committed to the Ongoing Life of the Church

First, the commitment of the individual vestry member to the ongoing life of the church is paramount. The vestry must embody the vision of the church. Parishioners will often use the commitment level of the vestry as a measure of their own commitment. For example, church members notice when vestry members are present or absent for major parish events. The absence of several vestry members from key events in the life of the congregation tells parishioners that their own attendance is not really important or necessary either.

33

If the event is considered a major parish event, all vestry members should be present (unless their absence is for good cause). If attendance is effectively optional for vestry members, the event should not be considered a major parish event. The congregation will often reflect the commitment level of the vestry. If the commitment level of individual vestry members is low, expect that same level of commitment among the congregation.

A common practice in churches is to nominate someone who is only marginally involved in the life of the parish in hopes that service on the vestry will make this person more committed. There are two flaws in this notion. First, it sends a signal to the congregation that commitment is really optional for service on the vestry. Second, the church now has some of the least committed people making major decisions on behalf of the congregation, people who may not know or embrace the real values of the congregation.

Past performance is the best indicator of future behavior. If you want a committed vestry, look for an already committed and active church member to serve on the vestry.

Committed to Participation in the Life of the Vestry

Second, the individual vestry member must be committed to the vestry leadership process. Each person must be a faithful and engaged member of the vestry. Serving on a vestry is not so much about making decisions as it is about forming community as the appropriate context for making the decisions that vestry members make. What is important is that each vestry member exhibit the highest commitment to be involved in vestry formation activities as well as vestry meetings.

For example, attendance at a vestry orientation or vestry planning retreat is a must. More than simply giving out information, this is a time of formation for the vestry as a community. Both in group sessions as well as during "down time," conversations, friendships, and working relationships are developed, as is group identity. When a vestry member misses an orientation or planning retreat, it often takes as long as six months for the missing vestry member to get back "up to speed" with the vestry as a whole. Often if there is a problem with the cohesiveness of the vestry, it is because of those who missed the orientation.

The business of a vestry is an ongoing conversation. Members who miss meetings are constantly having to be "brought up to speed" with the rest of the vestry and can be a drag on the cohesiveness and progress of the vestry.

Committed to the Financial Support of the Church

Finally, vestry members should be financially committed to the church commensurately with their ability to give.

Although the Episcopal Church has adopted the tithe as the standard of giving for faithful Episcopalians, not all have adopted this as a standard for their own parishioners and vestry members. The real issue for leadership in the church is not the dollar amount that one gives but the measure of faithfulness to the church.

Just as in the New Testament story the widow who gave her two mites was considered more faithful than the Pharisee who gave a larger sum of money but out of his excess, so the widow who gives sacrificially to the church might be a more faithful vestry member than the wealthy person who gives a mere pittance of his income.

I have often seen vestry members who are not financially committed become ongoing problems for the vestry. Here are the reasons:

- Those who are less than committed financially to the church will often be less than committed to other activities in the church's life. They seem to find it easier not to show up for major parish events.

- When it comes time to approve a budget or spending for a new initiative that requires faith that God will provide, the financially undercommitted vestry member is often reluctant to take the risk.

Putting it positively, when a person has given in a truly faithful way to the church, she will be more likely to believe that God will likewise faithfully provide for the church for its needs as well. Or, putting it negatively, because the vestry member has not given freely to the church, he will be similarly parsimonious when it comes to spending the church's money because he will assume that others are equally less committed.

It is often said that the church can rise no higher than the spiritual maturity of the rector or vicar. It is equally true that the church can rise no higher than the commitment level of the vestry. They set the standard, by their lifestyle, of what a committed member looks like.

For Individual or Group Reflection

- *On a scale of 1 to 10, with 1 being "not committed" and 10 being "fully committed," rate your own commitment to the life of your church, the vestry, and church finances.*

- *Using the same scale, how would the average church member rate your vestry?*

Seven

How to Conduct an
Effective Vestry Meeting

"A learning organization is one where people continually expand
their capacity to create the results they truly desire."
— *Peter Senge*

In chapter 3 we discussed the need for a good mental model for the
vestry. We showed the adversarial nature of the institutional model
for the vestry to be inappropriate and ineffective for a faith-based
community. We then proposed that a more appropriate model for the
vestry is that of a learning community. How does a vestry that wants
to be formed as a learning community actually conduct an effective
vestry meeting that does more than business as usual?

How to Lead an Ineffective Vestry Meeting

Most rectors and vicars inherit the "Approval of the Past Minutes
– Treasurer's Report – Old Business – New Business" approach to
agenda making. If you want to have really long meetings, use this
tried and tired method. Oh, and don't send out an agenda beforehand,
either. Instead, hand out the agenda at the beginning of the vestry
meeting; or, better yet, ask the vestry members at the beginning of the
meeting what should be on the agenda for that particular meeting.
This approach will guarantee a long and drawn out meeting where
much is discussed and probably very little accomplished.

There is a better way.

What the vestry does at the beginning of the meeting sets the tone
for the whole meeting. For example, the old "tried and tired" method

places maintenance issues at the beginning of the meeting with approval of the minutes and approval of the treasurer's report. So what you've done is devoted the high energy time of the meeting to the low energy issues. Also, when the vestry discusses the finances at the beginning of the meeting, you are telling the vestry that balancing the budget is really what is important in the life of the congregation. Most vestries, then, give their best energy and attention to the financial matters of the church and lose energy when it comes to the more important missional concerns.

There is a better way.

A Better Way:
How to Lead an Effective Vestry Meeting

Instead of the typical "Old Business–New Business" approach, John Maxwell of Injoy suggested to me an agenda with three sections: "Information–Discussion–Decision." I have added a fourth, Formation, and found this way of dealing with issues to be very effective.

First, **Formation** is the top priority for the vestry: being formed in Christian community. If your aim is to form the vestry as a community and further to form it as a learning community, then formation ought to be the priority at each meeting. A helpful acronym for vestry formation is VHS — Vision, Huddle, and Skill. I recommend thirty to forty-five minutes for formation. Then, the business part of the meeting can begin. It is important that this formation time not be considered optional. Don't excuse people for being late on a regular basis. Formation is job one of the vestry.

Second, **Information** is just that: information that needs no discussion or decision by the vestry: keeping people in the loop on pertinent information. This section includes items such as new members, upcoming events of note, announcement of new staff members or administrative issues. You're not asking the vestry to discuss or decide anything; you're just keeping them informed about what's happening in the life of the congregation.

Third, **Discussion** covers issues for which you want to receive feedback or to do some brainstorming, but about which the vestry is not ready to decide. I strongly recommend that nothing be presented to the vestry for an immediate decision without having been discussed the month prior. To engage in discussion without pressing for a decision allows for a much freer exchange of ideas and concerns. People can discuss an issue without feeling the pressure of having to convince others right on the spot. Here the pastor can elicit feedback on questions like the newcomers' ministry, the need to add another staff member, challenges facing the congregation or diocese, or larger projects that will be decided by the vestry at a later date.

The fourth area of the agenda is *Decision.* Only after an issue has been discussed by the vestry at the prior month's meeting should it be brought before the vestry for a decision — unless it is a "slam dunk" or an emergency, and there are very few of those. The presumption is that nothing is voted on unless it has been on the Discussion agenda for at least a month. Generally, the Decision part of the agenda will have the fewest items. You'll also find that by using this approach to setting the agenda, the Decision-making items take up the least amount of time, because all of the discussion will already have taken place, and most of the energy will have been given to missional rather than maintenance matters. Wise pastors will know not to put anything on the Decision agenda unless they already know the outcome.

Another point should be made about the month (at least) between the time that an item is put on the Discussion part of the agenda and the time for making a Decision: the pastor and wardens should spend that month talking to vestry members, listening and addressing concerns, convincing where appropriate, being willing to change because of collaboration. The pastor should not miss the "pre-meeting meeting" where this particular issue is discussed. Again, wise pastors will not put anything on the Decision agenda unless they already know the outcome.

Finally, after the teaching, sharing, or worship time of formation, after providing information, and after non-hurried discussion about the life of the congregation, and after the usually non-argumentative decision-making time — now comes the treasurer's report. Placing the treasurer's report at the end of the meeting has several effects. First, it emphasizes that finances follow mission and vision rather than determining mission and vision. This gives the vestry appropriate time to exercise its responsibility as fiduciary agents on behalf of the congregation rather than having the financial discussions be the engine that drives the vestry meeting, overshadowing discussion of the mission of the church. Second, after spending all that time and energy on these other issues, vestry members are usually too tired to fuss much about finances. (I say this only partially in jest.)

The purpose of this approach is not to stifle discussion but to enhance it, not to hide information from the vestry but to make it more available. Think of the difference between an incandescent light bulb and a laser. An incandescent light bulb spreads light in all directions. A laser focuses and concentrates light to perform a variety of tasks from pointing to making incisions for surgery. Providing people with timely information and freedom of discussion without prematurely forcing a decision helps decision-makers really process the information, makes them feel as though they've truly been heard, and ultimately draws the vestry together collaboratively. This approach focuses light on each item in a more laser-like way that utilizes members' time more effectively, keeps the agenda in a logical sequence, and helps everyone focus energy on what is truly important and not just on the immediate emotional topics of one or two individuals.

Preparing the Agenda

Now, let's turn to how to prepare the agenda.

First, the agenda and the treasurer's report should be distributed to the vestry members a week in advance of the meeting. No new item of business can be placed on the agenda once it has been mailed out, unless it is an emergency (and there should be very few emergencies). Spur-of-the-moment discussions make for long meetings and can derail an otherwise productive meeting. Remember that nothing is put on the Decision agenda without having been on the Discussion agenda the month before.

Second, individual financial questions should be addressed to the treasurer ahead of the meeting. When asking a financial question the guiding principle should be: Is this information for the good of the vestry as a whole, or is it simply based on my need to know or my need for clarification? St. Paul might ask, "Is the whole body edified by the question?" If it is simply motivated by my need to know, that question can be asked before the meeting. Exercising one's fiduciary responsibility does not give people the right to micromanage the finances.

Third, prepare an agenda with clear time allocation. As part of the agenda, make three columns: Item discussed, with a brief description of what is at issue; who is presenting; and the estimated time it should take. This gives the vestry a preview of the meeting and an idea of how long the meeting should last. It communicates that the agenda has been thoughtfully prepared and that they can expect a productive meeting. On the following page is a sample agenda for a 2 hour and 15 minute meeting.

Is it realistic to expect that the time frames will be accurate? No. Some items will go over, while others may take less time. The important thing is that it gives the vestry members an indication of what is on the agenda, the amount of time the vestry can expect each item to require, and when vestry members may reasonably expect the meeting to end.

This approach to agenda-making may seem at first to be too highly structured and controlling. This is where the art of leadership comes into play. Time estimates are a guide to give vestry members an indication of the relative importance of the respective items. Kevin Martin, dean of St. Matthew's Cathedral in Dallas, Texas, says that no good vestry decisions are made after 9:00 p.m.

For Individual or Group Reflection

* *Reflect on your previous vestry meetings. How much time was spent discussing certain issues? Was this time well spent relative to the importance of the issue being discussed?*

* *Which part of a typical vestry meeting do you get the most meaning from? Why?*

St. Somewhere's Episcopal Church Vestry Agenda February 29, 2004 – 7:00 p.m.		
Item	Presenter	Estimated Time
Teaching — "Sizing up the Congregation"	Fr. Neal	45 min.
Information		
Approval of Minutes	Fr. Neal	15 min.
Staff Retreat — Wed., March 6, 2004; led by Canon Martin	Fr. Neal	
VBS Training — Sat., March 20	Fr. Neal	
Diocesan Stewardship Workshop, Sat., Apr. 23, 2004 — All vestry members are expected to attend	Hunt C.	
Bishop's Visitation — May 26, 8:00 a.m. and 10:30 a.m. Dinner with vestry, Sat., May 25, 6:30 p.m. — RSVP to Colleen B.	Fr. Neal	
Mission trip to Honduras — 23 from SSEC — See handout	Fr. Neal	
Discussion		
Review of Newcomers' Orientation Process Recent changes to Newcomers' course, length, additions to process	Alethia A.	15 min.
Discussion of changing youth position to full-time	Fr. Neal	15 min.
Discussion of whether to host a Faith Alive	Fr. Neal Tom L.	25 min.
Decision		
Land acquisition — Letter of intent to purchase two-acre strip of land across back of property — See handout from January meeting	Hylmar K.	10 min.
Aspirant for Holy Orders Chris Roque seeks vestry approval — See handout	Fr. Neal	5 min.
Treasurer's Report	John M.	5 min.
Prayer		

Eight

Other Means for Forming a Vestry as a Learning Community

"Tinker to Evers to Chance"
— *Chicago Cubs double play combination from 1903 to 1910;*
immortalized in a poem by New York sportswriter
Franklin P. Adams

Forming the vestry as a learning community requires more than just reworking the vestry meeting format. Besides the vestry meeting, attention should also be paid to the vestry selection process, vestry orientation, the vestry retreat, and teachable moments.

Vestry Selection Process

Many churches have a "y'all come" approach to vestry elections: almost anybody will do as long as they are warm bodies and communicants in good standing. Often churches will list the bare minimum canonical requirements for eligibility to serve as a vestry member. When churches have minimal eligibility requirements, they often get minimal leaders. Parish leadership, however, is too important to be content with minimal commitment.

A better approach is to build certain minimal requirements and commitments appropriate to your local context beyond the minimum canonical requirements for a person to be nominated to serve on the vestry. Remember that past performance is the best indicator of future behavior. If you want leaders on the vestry, solicit candidates who have demonstrated leadership and commitment to the church.

For example, consider requiring vestry nominees to be committed to tithe or to commit to tithing within three years. Also, involvement in Sunday school or a Bible study or small group or ministry group should be required of each vestry nominee. Does your church have a vision statement or long-range plan or a history of the church that could be read before a person agrees to be nominated? Finally, expectations concerning attendance at vestry meetings, vestry orientation, and the annual vestry retreat should be agreed to before a person's name is placed in nomination.

Finally, as a part of the interview and recruitment process for prospective vestry members, have the person who is soliciting a nominee be ready to discuss these questions with the prospective nominee:

* What does this prospective nominee "bring to the table"? Does this person have particular knowledge or background needed by the vestry? Is the prospective nominee a long-standing member or a newcomer who will bring a different perspective? If the prospective nominee has a background similar to the other vestry members, it may be better to look further afield.

* What has the vestry accomplished in the past three years that makes vestry service attractive? Are the meetings maintenance-driven or missionally oriented? Low energy or high energy?

* What type of person would want to serve on this vestry? Would a certain type of person be frustrated?

* Will this prospective nominee talk to three or four current vestry members before consenting to be nominated? The nominee should know what service on the vestry is really like before consenting to be nominated.

Vestry Orientation

Critical to the formation of any vestry is a time at the beginning of the year when new members come on board to provide an orientation for its members. This should not be just for the new members but for all the members. This insures that each vestry member will be "reading on the same page."

Some previously oriented vestry members will complain, "I went to that last year." Good. They can help orient the new members. They can evaluate the orientation in light of their previous experience. The vestry orientation is not just a time for giving the new members information; it is a time for forming the vestry as a community.

Some churches will begin the year with a vestry planning retreat. This is absolutely the worst time for a planning retreat. Holding the planning retreat at the beginning of the year requires that new members — who have not yet been formed as a vestry, who don't know how the vestry functions, who have no awareness of the corporate memory nor acknowledgment of the values of the congregation — to try to discern God's direction for the congregation. A vestry planning retreat is better held in the middle of the year, after the vestry has learned, prayed, and played together for six months.

A better approach is to begin the year with a vestry orientation retreat. This should be held away from the church and in facilities that are at least as good as your church has. I once held a vestry orientation retreat in a church that had just built a new educational and administrative building. Our own facilities were in need of sprucing up because of deferred maintenance; their new facilities spoke volumes to our vestry of the need for excellence.

Four areas should be dealt with at a vestry orientation:

1. *Community formation.* Community formation is priority number one. The vestry is not just a board of directors casting votes and making decisions. It is involved in the spiritual leadership of the church. Trust takes time to develop among the individual vestry members. Allow time for the sharing of individuals' spiritual journeys as well as their understanding of their own role on the vestry at this time.

2. *Canonical requirements.* We are a church under authority: the authority of our bishop and of our denominational and diocesan canons as well as locally adopted policies and bylaws. The vestry needs to know what the various canons require of it.

3. *Vision, mission, and values of the local congregation.* How would you answer the question of what makes this congregation unique?

Why are you asking these good people to sacrifice their time, talent, and treasure on behalf of this congregation?

4. ***The role of the vestry member and how the vestry functions as a group.*** What are the roles of the different officers? Does the vestry operate by consensus or majority? Robert's *Rules of Order*? Are there attendance requirements, Sunday responsibilities, liaison obligations, or other commitments for people to place on their calendars during the upcoming year?

Churches that begin the year with this type of vestry orientation tend to have a much more effective and harmonious year. Those vestry members that miss the orientation spend most of the year "catching up" with the vestry, a step behind in relationships, and not fully conversant with the direction that the vestry is going. For them it is like joining midway through a conversation.

Vestry Retreat

Even with a vestry using the meeting format as proposed in this book, monthly vestry meetings can still seem like "business as usual." A vestry retreat can provide a time apart for the vestry for spiritual nourishment and refreshment. This is a time for further community building, vision-casting, teaching, and sharing. In addition, the vestry retreat can be a time of reviewing major planning and capital campaign plans. Depending on the need of the vestry at the time, the focus can be on spiritual development, planning, or relational issues among the vestry.

When planning for this vestry retreat, the leaders should ask what the critical issues are facing the vestry and the congregation. Have they already identified goals and directions that they want to accomplish in the coming year? This will provide the content for some of the time together.

The vestry retreat can be held with or apart from the vestry orientation, but it should be held away from the church to give the vestry members a fresh perspective in their conversations. Further, an overnight vestry retreat allows for conversations and establishing relationships that are just not possible in a one-day retreat.

Teachable Moments

Alastor ("Mad-Eye") Moody in the Harry Potter books gives excellent advice to leaders when he repeatedly says to those around him, "Constant vigilance!" Forming a vestry as a learning community means that the leader is constantly vigilant in noticing and taking advantage of teachable moments that arise from time to time. A teachable moment occurs in the course of a meeting, a conversation, or a class when the hearer is able to learn in a new and fresh way in response to an immediate event or comment. These might be called "Aha! moments." Hearers get a new insight that they might not be expecting at that moment. Vestry meetings provide a regular supply of teachable moments.

Jesus used teachable moments all the time. Consider when he says, "It is easier for a camel to go through the eye of a needle than for someone who is rich to enter the kingdom of God" (Matt 19:24, NRSV). Some scholars have speculated that this saying might have originated with Jesus pointing out to his hearers a camel trying to enter through a local gate in Jerusalem called "the eye of a needle."

I know of a rector who serves a church with an Anglo congregation and a Spanish-language congregation that share facilities. Although both groups are committed to each other and committed to being one church, the actual working out of that commitment has been difficult at times. Recently the congregation sent a team made up of members of both congregations on a short-term mission trip to Peru. The members of the Spanish-speaking congregation served as translators for the Anglos as they shared common tasks on the trip.

When the team returned from their mission trip, they gave a report to the congregation. As they shared their experiences, the team members wept and embraced. The rector then commented to the congregation, "Isn't it interesting that all the years of tension between the two congregations has been transcended by these members leaving their familiar surroundings and engaging in ministry together on this mission trip?"

That was a teachable moment. The rector responded to the moment, didn't overemphasize the point, and moved on.

Leaders must be aware of those teachable moments with their vestry — and all other groups as well — and turn each subcommunity into a learning community.

For Individual or Group Reflection

- *When you first served on a board of directors or the vestry, how long did it take for you to "get up to speed"?*

- *If you are a veteran vestry member, what do you know now that you wish someone had told you when you first agreed to serve on the vestry?*

— Nine —

Urgency and Non-Anxious Presence in Healthy Tension

"What, me worry?"
— Mad *Magazine's Alfred E. Newman*

One of the great challenges for the church leader is dealing with the issue of urgency. John Kotter, in *Leading Change* (Harvard Business School Press, 1996), identifies ten reasons why transformation efforts fail. One of those is the failure to establish a sense of urgency.

Psychologists distinguish between good stress and bad stress. Much of the stress that we want to alleviate is considered bad stress. If one loses one's job, experiences the death of a loved one, and moves to a new community — all in the same year — this will amount to bad stress in an individual's life. On the other hand, the threat of receiving a grade of "F" can be good stress that will motivate a student to study or to finish an assignment on time.

Similarly, there is good urgency, and there is bad urgency. Some kinds of urgency will be harmful to a church; other kinds will be helpful. Effective leadership is about distinguishing between these two kinds of urgency, artfully minimizing bad urgency and fostering good urgency as a positive motivation.

Tyranny of the Urgent

When I was in college, I read a little pamphlet that changed my life. It was *Tyranny of the Urgent* by Charles Hummel (InterVarsity Press, 1967). Tyranny of the Urgent is when we are so carried away by what is urgent that the individual or organization doesn't have the time or the focus to deal with what is truly important. As the *Washington*

49

Post fretted in a review about one of the Harry Potter books: "We are slaves to the Next."

A church that spends all its energy focusing on the "urgent," the "Next," can be very debilitating. It develops an attitude of frustration as it trudges from one crisis to another. The vestry functions in a continual crisis mode and leaves members exhausted when their terms expire. I have known vestry members who marked the calendar much like prison inmates waiting for their sentences to end. Nor is it uncommon for former vestry members and wardens to spend at least their first year away from church, recuperating from their time of service on the vestry.

Service on the vestry gets a reputation for being drudgery. When this happens it becomes increasingly difficult to recruit good nominees to serve on the vestry. (Sometimes it is difficult to recruit even bad nominees to serve on the vestry.) Over time, a debilitating complacency sets in among the vestry as well as in the church.

Right Urgency as the Antidote to Complacency

However, not all urgency is bad. The kind of urgency that John Kotter identifies is an urgency that moves people from a debilitating complacency to embrace change for the good of the organization. When complacency is high, few people are interested in cooperating to effect the helpful change. Likewise, when complacency is high, the small things get overlooked, you won't get people to go the extra mile, and morale is eroded.

Take Home Depot, for example. When Robert Nardelli became the CEO of Home Depot, he took over a business that was entrepreneurial in the extreme. It was on a tremendous growth curve, but he and the board of directors recognized that the practices that had brought Home Depot its success would not serve it well in the future. Each store had developed an independent mind-set; and Home Depot had become, not a particular brand with certain expectations that the customer could rely on from store to store, but a collection of individual stores.

Through a variety of tools and training, Nardelli established a sense of urgency that brought health to the company. It ultimately reaped the advantages of its size and served the consumer even more effectively, while at the same time making its employees happier and more fulfilled.

Nardelli would hold store managers accountable for increases or decreases in sales, profitability, and so on. Store managers would point to individual stories of tremendous customer satisfaction while the overall sales and profits in their stores were in decline. Nardelli would not accept only anecdotal evidence that Home Depot customers at a particular store were generally happy; he also held those store managers accountable by quantitative measures. Kotter calls this use of anecdotal stories "happy talk." Leaders are sometimes very good at "happy talk" while the organization is really in decline. Remember the story of the emperor's new clothes.

Robert Nardelli established a sense of urgency among the store managers and the organization as a whole by focusing on the hard data of profit and loss.

Non-Anxious Presence

We have seen that it can be debilitating when organizations focus their energy only on urgency. Those organizations that establish a sense of urgency also need for their leaders to be non-anxious presences in the midst of the changes. However, some people who think that they are being a non-anxious presence might, in fact, be in denial or clueless. Nardelli showed that for an organization to depend only on anecdotal evidence to communicate how the organization is doing can lead to a skewed picture of how the organization is really doing.

A survey of the Episcopal Church from a couple of years ago, "Faith Communities Today," asked congregations to complete a survey that asked questions similar to those found on their parochial reports (the annual reporting that each congregation sends to the diocese, covering such statistics as membership, average Sunday attendance, income, and so on). When the compilers of the survey compared the completed surveys with those of that congregation's parochial reports, it was obvious that in many instances the survey results contradicted the parochial report data. Only those churches that were growing 10 percent or more per year "told the truth." The vast majority of churches reported that they were doing better than their parochial reports indicated. Happy talk.

There is a difference between happy talk and being a non-anxious presence. What did Nardelli do? He raised the level of urgency while at the same time he instituted changes and provided training, consolidation, and communication (transparency). Basically he put a system in place that modeled the preferable behaviors. He was a non-anxious presence in the midst of the changes that he was proposing. He was not a non-anxious presence with respect to the complacency that had overtaken the company. Instead, he held in a healthy tension the polar opposites of establishing a sense of urgency with being a non-anxious presence in the midst of that necessary urgency and attendant change.

Being a Non-Anxious Presence Is Not Simply a Technique

Of course, being a non-anxious presence is not simply a leadership technique. If your soul is frenetic, anxious, and striving, no amount of relaxation will make you a non-anxious presence.

To be a non-anxious presence in the midst of major change has two requirements. First, it calls for the leader to have a compelling vision of where the organization is headed. Without a vision to guide the organization, all changes are equal in value and priority. Proposed changes must be in service of the vision. The leader who has no vision for the future of the organization may not be able to withstand the lonely days and nights when resistance comes — as it most certainly will.

Second, to be a non-anxious presence requires a soul to be at peace. Thus, it is important that the leader maintain a healthy spiritual life. This is done through practicing the spiritual disciplines so that the leader's soul is truly at peace, regardless of the circumstances. What is at the bottom of your soul? Are you comfortable with silence? If we are listening to too many voices, we are unable to hear the "still, small voice of calm" in solitude.

Some Suggestions

Among the things that the non-anxious change agent can do are the following:

+ *Be transparent and keep the lines of communication open.* Kevin Martin, dean of St. Matthew's Cathedral in Dallas, sends out a regular e-mail to the leaders in that parish. He began with the vestry and an invitation for any in the parish who considered themselves leaders to subscribe. He discusses upcoming events and their significance for the cathedral; he floats ideas and elicits feedback. People at the cathedral really feel informed about what's going on.

+ *Provide training for the preferred methods of behavior.* People don't automatically "get it" when they're told the first time. They need time to absorb the changes. Give them time, but provide training so that there are no surprises.

+ *Reward positive performers.* What gets rewarded gets done. How are you rewarding those people who do seem to "get it" and are doing it? It may be something as little as a thank-you note or a special treat.

+ *Celebrate successes.* But remember, they must be true successes. Small successes added to small successes turn into momentum.

+ *Listen to those most affected by the changes.* Don't take opposition or reluctance personally. Most people simply want to be heard. A simple way of helping people know that they've been heard is for you to repeat what they said back to them. The old Rogerian maxim "What I hear you saying is . . ." is a good practice.

For Individual or Group Reflection

+ *What motivates your stewardship program? Is it to maintain the status quo? keep the ministries at their current levels? maintain the facilities? Or do you motivate the congregation through missional opportunities?*

+ *When did the church last launch a ministry that it couldn't really afford but did so because the leadership believed that God was calling them to do so?*

+ *What are people most urgent about in your congregation?*

Part Two

Exercises for Moving Beyond Business as Usual

Why Four Types of Resources?

This section has four types of resources: Bible Studies, Teachings, Mental Exercises, and Reflective Readings. We use different kinds of resources because different people process information and learn in different ways.

Introverts tend to be more reflective in processing information, while others may be more linear in their logic. To quote Sergeant Joe Friday of the old *Dragnet* series: some want "just the facts, Ma'am." Auditory learners prefer to listen to someone teach rather than read the material for themselves. Others are visual learners. Charts and diagrams help them learn. Some people relish having notes and an outline and love an outline that allows them to "fill-in-the-blanks." This approach allows them to interact with the material and the speaker. Still others, kinesthetic learners, learn best when physically involved with the material.

Therefore some of the Bible Studies are more reflective in nature while others aim at eliciting specific lessons from the text. Some Mental Exercises call for reflection while others require a certain amount of activity and information. The Reflective Readings don't provide information as much as they call for people to think through issues. The Teachings tend to be more informational and linear, conveying information otherwise not known to the vestry member.

If you use only one style to convey information, you may be missing a significant part of your vestry, as some may have a learning style that engages them in a way other than the style that you happen to favor.

Four Ways to Use These Resources

1. Have the vestry members read and discuss one chapter a month over a nine-month period. Each chapter ends with some questions to help facilitate discussion.

2. Assign a chapter to be summarized by a different vestry member each session and have that person lead the discussion. Being

responsible for teaching the material and leading the discussion
is a good way to have the individual "own" the material.

3. Hold a vestry retreat during which the vestry reads and discusses
   each chapter in thirty-minute segments.

4. Use individual resources each month based on the specialized
   needs of your individual vestry. Reflect on chapter 5: "Discerning
   Your Vestry's Pinch Points." Select those resources that will allow
   the vestry to focus on the specific pinch point that they need to
   work on.

Here are some themes you can focus on while using these resources
in clusters.

Relationships

+ *Icebreaker #1 or #2* (Mental Exercise, page 101)

+ *Doing the Right Thing or Doing the Thing Right,* 2 Samuel 6:1–7
  (Bible Study, page 63)

+ *Unity,* John 17:20–23 (Bible Study, page 65)

+ *Four Principles Every Church Leader Should Take to Heart* (Teaching,
  page 69)

+ *How to Boil an Egg* (Reflective Reading, page 115)

+ *The Timeline of My Life* (Mental Exercise, page 108)

Congregational Development

+ *What Do These Numbers Mean?* (Mental Exercise, page 109)

+ *Is St. Swithin's a Five-Star Church?* (Mental Exercise, page 102)

+ *Mission,* The Book of Acts (Bible Study, page 65)

+ *Vision*, Acts 1:1–11 (Bible Study, page 66)

+ *Lay Leadership,* Acts 6:1–7 (Bible Study, page 67)

+ *Congregational Development According to Yogi* (Teaching, page 80)

+ *Introduction to Congregational Size Dynamics* (Teaching, page 83)

+ *Mystery Worshipper* (Mental Exercise, page 105)

Administrative Pinchpoints

+ *Icebreaker Question #2* (Mental Exercise, page 101)

+ *Doing the Right Thing or Doing the Thing Right,* 1 Samuel 6:1–7 (Bible Study, page 63)

+ *Thinking Like a Leader* (Teaching, page 75)

+ *Why Organizations Fail* (Teachings, page 97)

+ *Is St. Swithin's a Five-Star Church?* (Mental Exercise, page 102)

+ *What Do These Numbers Mean?* (Mental Exercise, page 109)

+ *What Drives Your Church?* (Reflective Reading, page 111)

Spiritual Pinchpoints

+ *Icebreaker Question #2* (Mental Exercise, page 101)

+ *The Timeline of My Life* (Mental Exercise, page 108)

+ *Leadership,* Exodus 18:13–27 (Bible Study, page 62)

+ *Lay Leadership,* Acts 6:1–7 (Bible Study, page 67)

+ *Four Principles Every Church Leader Should Take to Heart* (Teaching, page 69)

+ *The Crucible of Leadership* (Reflective Reading, page 113)

+ *In Praise of Passion* (Reflective Reading, page 120)

Sample Ten-Month Vestry Teaching Schedule

1. Bible Study — Acts 6:1–11 (see page 67)

2. Thinking Like a Leader (see page 75)

3. Why Organizations Fail (see page 97)

4. Exercise — Is St. Swithin's a Five-Star Church? (see page 102)

5. Congregational Size Dynamics (see page 83)

6. Congregational Life Cycle (see Neal Michell, *How to Hit the Ground Running: A Quick Start Quide to Congregations with New Leadership,* pp. 17–22)

7. Moving from Solitude to Community to Ministry (see page 73)

8. History of St. Swithin's — Growth, Giving, and Gesticulations of St. Swithin's

9. Demographics (see *http://episcopalchurch.org* for demographic material for zip codes in which Episcopal churches are located)

10. Mental Exercise: St. Swithin's is a _____ -Driven Church (see page 111)

Ten

Bible Studies

Blessed Lord, who caused all holy Scriptures to be written for our learning: Grant us so to hear them, read, mark, learn, and inwardly digest them, that we may embrace and ever hold fast the blessed hope of everlasting life, which you have given us in our Savior Jesus Christ; who lives and reigns with you and the Holy Spirit, one God, for ever and ever. Amen.

Whether they were Celtic Christians in the British Isles or people of the Reformation, Anglicans have long held a love for the Scriptures and the aim to be formed by the Scriptures. These Bible studies focus primarily on leadership issues. Sometimes new vestry members don't have an appreciation of the shift in thinking that must take place at the leadership level. These studies can be beneficial for the vestry at any time, or they can be used in a retreat setting to aid in a discussion among vestry members to leadership and its unique responsibilities and opportunities.

Bible Study 1
Theme: Leadership
Passage: Exodus 18:13–27

Here we find Moses exhausted...and the people are exhausted...because Moses is trying to do too much by himself. That is a weakness in many really competent people: they have a hard time letting anyone else do anything because no one else can do it as well. Meanwhile, the "to-do" list gets longer and longer and things don't get done well because there is too much for one individual to do. Training others takes time, but it is time well spent that will eventually multiply the leader.

Read Exodus 18:13–27 and then discuss the following questions:.

1. What was the problem (v. 13)?

2. What were the ramifications of the problem (vv. 17–18)?

3. Who came up with the solution (vv. 17–19)?

4. What was the solution (vv. 19–21)?

5. How were the leaders trained (v. 20)?

6. What do we learn about leadership from this passage?

Bible Study 2
Theme: Doing the Right Thing or Doing the Thing Right
Passage: 2 Samuel 6:1–7

This passage is more than a bit troubling. Our modern sensibilities tend to want to tame the God of the Old Testament. Nevertheless, this story presents a valuable lesson for all leaders.

Read 2 Samuel 6:1–7 and then discuss the following questions:

1. Why is the ark being moved at this time? (You'll have to do some background reading to answer this question.)

2. Why is Uzzah's act considered "irreverent" (vv. 6–7; compare Exodus 25:12–14)?

3. When have you ever tried to do the right thing but did it the wrong way? What were the consequences?

Bible Study 3
Theme: The Leader's Priorities
Passage: Ezra 7:8–10

This short passage carries a powerful lesson for the leader in the church. Ezra was given a challenging task, but, as this passage says, "the hand of the Lord was upon him," in other words, God blessed him. This passage gives us the order of priorities in leadership.

Read Ezra 7:8–10 and then discuss the following questions:

1. Why was the hand of the Lord upon Ezra (v. 9)?
2. What were his priorities (v. 10)?

   For the leader:

   a. Ezra devoted himself to the study of the "Law of the Lord."
   b. Ezra lived it out himself.
   c. Ezra then taught others what he had learned.

Bible Study 4
Theme: Leadership and Loneliness
Passage: Luke 22:39–46

At times all leaders feel like they're all alone. Sometimes circumstances justify that feeling, and sometimes they do not. The higher the risk, the greater the sense of loneliness can be. Jesus' praying in the Garden of Gethsemane is a comfort to all leaders during those times when they feel that no one is with them.

Read Luke 22:39–46 and then discuss the following questions:

1. In times of crisis, where do you go to "get away from it all"?
2. Why would Jesus ask his disciples to pray that they not enter into temptation (vv. 39–40)?
3. How must Jesus have felt when he moved away from the disciples (v. 41)?
4. When Jesus says, "Your will be done," is his attitude one of:

   • complacency, whatever will be will be, and I can't do anything about it? Or
   • trusting resignation, knowing that his heavenly Father cared for him?

5. What was God's response to Jesus' honesty?

6. How did Jesus respond?

Bible Study 5
Theme: Unity
Passage: John 17:20–23

This passage comes from what has been called the "High Priestly Prayer of Jesus." The setting is in the Garden of Gethsemane during Holy Week just before Jesus is arrested and crucified. These words are among his final words and express his real concern for those disciples who would follow him.

Read John 17:20–23 and then discuss the following questions

1. For whom is Jesus praying here (v. 20)?

2. What is he asking for (v. 21)?

3. What characterizes those who will follow Jesus (v. 22)?

4. What is the basis for our unity (v. 22)?

5. What will be the result of our unity (v. 23)?

6. What obstacles to unity do we find in our church? our vestry?

Bible Study 6
Theme: Mission
Passage: Book of Acts

Clay Lein, rector of St. Philip's Episcopal Church in Frisco, Texas, says that his responsibility as rector is to keep the vestry focused on mission. For several years he has led his vestry at each vestry meeting to study passages from the book of Acts.

Read a passage from the book of Acts and then discuss the following questions:

1. Where is mission in this passage?

2. What are the obstacles to mission in this passage?

3. What necessities for mission do we find here?

4. What is God saying to us out of this?

Bible Study 7
Theme: Vision
Passage: Acts 1:1–11

Vision is crucial for any organization: "Where there is no vision the people perish" (Prov 29:18, KJV). Or, as Yogi Berra said, "You got to be careful if you don't know where you're going, because you might not get there." Without vision the organization will limp into the future. As the NIV translation for Proverbs 29:18 emphasizes — "Where there is no vision the people cast off restraint" — vision will keep people focused. Without a vision anything that anyone wants to do in an organization is permissible. Without a vision, the loudest voice will generally carry the day in any leadership group.

Read Acts 1:1–11. In this passage we see that vision:

1. comes from *God*

2. to a *particular people*

3. in a *particular setting*

4. at a *particular time*

5. for a *particular work.*

Pass out index cards. Have all the participants write out what their vision of the church is on their card. The cards need not be signed. After several minutes the leader should read aloud each vision statement.

Questions to ask:

1. Do these vision statements have any common elements or themes?

2. Are any of them particularly out of sync with the others? (A lack of similarity will indicate a lack of agreement about the vision of the church and indicates that much work needs to be done in discerning, articulating, and continually communicating the vision.)

<u>Bible Study 8</u>
Theme: Lay Leadership
Passage: Acts 6:1–7

Acts 6 describes one of the first challenges in the early church where the demands for ministry were greater than the capacity of the leaders to meet those needs personally. (Note to leader: In this instance it was the apostles who were the leaders. In discussing the apostles' response, be careful not to read our current views of diaconal ordination into this passage. When the apostles decided to raise up deacons for ministry, they were not developing a new category of ordained persons. They were raising up lay leaders to fulfill the ministry needs in the early church.)

Read Acts 6:1–7 and then discuss the following questions:

1. What was the problem facing the early church (v. 1)?

2. What was their solution (vv. 2–4)?

3. What qualities were they looking for in these new leaders (v. 3)?

4. How did the apostles acknowledge that these should be recognized as leaders in the church (v. 6)?

5. What was the result of raising up new (lay) leaders in the church (v. 7)?

6. On a scale of 1 to 10, is our church more lay driven (1) or clergy driven (10)?

— Eleven —

Teachings

Almighty God, you have built your church upon the foundation of the apostles and prophets, Jesus Christ himself being the chief cornerstone: Grant us so to be joined together in unity of spirit by their teaching that we may be made a holy temple acceptable to you; through Jesus Christ our Lord, who lives and reigns with you and the Holy Spirit, one God, for ever and ever. Amen.

Some information just has to be communicated and studied. These Teachings focus primarily on congregational development issues. They are designed to help vestry members to begin thinking of the church as an organization and reflect on the church from a consultant's perspective. There is a saying, "You can't see the forest for the trees." Often vestry members get so involved in the individual parts of the congregation (the trees) that they fail to appreciate the larger picture of the congregation (the forest). Studying these teachings will help vestry members to appreciate that many of the issues that their church faces are neither unusual nor peculiar only to them.

Pay particular attention to the section on congregational size dynamics. These materials will help vestry members see that some of the issues facing their congregation are really theologically neutral. The best way to use these lessons is to present the "Introduction to Congregational Size Dynamics" (see page 83) and then to present the materials on a church smaller than their own church and then the next larger size, and then finally their own size. Vestry members will see the implications of the size of their own congregation.

<u>Teaching 1</u>
Four Principles Every Church Leader
Should Take to Heart

Often in churches, new vestry members don't initially understand or appreciate the increased responsibilities that come with serving on the vestry. They often see themselves as parishioners who have been elected or appointed to a new position rather than leaders with increased responsibilities to the organization. Here are four principles that new (and continuing) vestry members ought to know that will save the church much grief if they are, indeed, taken to heart. Principles 1, 2, and 4 come from John Maxwell of Injoy. Number 3 on triangulation comes from Kevin Martin, dean of St. Matthew's Episcopal Cathedral in Dallas, Texas.

1. The Relationship between Rights and Responsibilities

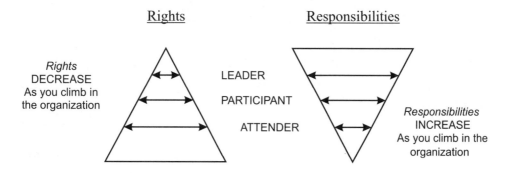

Churches generally have three types of people: Attenders, Participants, and Leaders.

* *Attenders* show up when they want, and no more is expected of them.

* *Participants* have certain responsibilities on behalf of the organization.

* *Leaders* have responsibility for people in the organization.

As the person moves from being an Attender to being a Participant to being a Leader, he or she acquires increased responsibilities. Along with growth in responsibility comes the giving up of certain rights. The surrendering of rights is part of growth in responsibility.

Two more points:

- Leaders are to live by a higher standard than followers (by virtue of greater responsibility).

- The higher the leader climbs in the organization, the less lateral movement there is.

The higher the leaders climb in the organization, the greater their responsibilities and the fewer their rights.

2. The Fire Brigade

In every church there are always little fires erupting: someone gets upset, someone's feelings get hurt, conflicts occur. What is the leader's responsibility with respect to the fire?

In the church, each one of us carries around two buckets: one is full of water and one is full of gasoline. What happens to the fire depends on which bucket we pour on the fire. If we throw water on the fire, it helps put out the fire. If we throw gasoline on the fire, the fire will only blaze higher and hotter.

The leader never has the right to throw gasoline on any church fire.

3. The Favoritest Game in the Church: Triangulation

In human interactive terms, a triangle occurs when each of two opposing parties seeks to join with a third party against the other, with the third party finding it necessary to cooperate now with one and now with another of these opposing parties.

The diagram on the following page shows what triangulation looks like. It works like this:

A has a grievance against **C** (whether valid or invalid), but instead of going directly to **C**, **A** instead talks to **B** about it.

A wants **B** to confront **C** but without telling **C** that it is **A** who has the grievance.

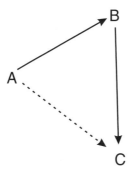

In this scenario, **A** wields power over **C** (unidentified discontent) and **B** (manipulation). **B** wields power over **C** because for **C** to get a resolution with **A**, **C** must go through **B**.

How to handle triangulation:

1. **B** should encourage **A** to talk to **C** and state her concerns personally.

2. Alternatively, **B** should lovingly tell **A** that he will go with her to **C,** or that **B** will be happy to convey **A**'s concerns to **C** but that **B** will need to reveal **A**'s identity to **C** because he is sure that **C** will want to discuss these concerns with **A**. In any event, **B** should not carry **A**'s message anonymously.

3. Lay the ground rules, stating that we don't communicate anonymous messages. Period. If **A** wishes to remain anonymous, the complaint goes unreported.

Healthy leaders never play the triangulation game.

4. Always Communicate Upstream

Anytime someone has a complaint or a concern, it must always be sent "upstream" where it can be resolved. Imagine that a person with a complaint is alongside a stream. The water purification plant is located upstream. The village is located downstream. One person complaining to another is pollution. Sending the complaint downstream (simply repeated to anybody and everybody) is tantamount to pouring contaminated water into the stream where it will flow downstream and pollute the village. If the complaint is sent upstream (for example, to the vestry or the staff, where it can be resolved), that is like sending it to the water purification plant, where it can be purified and flow downstream and not contaminate the village.

The vestry member or congregational leader must never communicate complaints or conflicts downstream where it sows discord among the community and will pollute the congregation. The issue for the leader: do you want to fix the problem, or do you just want to talk about it? If you only want to talk about it, you are part of the problem; whereas sending the complaint upstream allows the complainer to be a part of the solution.

> *There are six things that the Lord hates,*
> *   seven that are an abomination to him:*
> *haughty eyes, a lying tongue,*
> *   and hands that shed innocent blood,*
> *a heart that devises wicked plans,*
> *   feet that hurry to run to evil,*
> *a lying witness who testifies falsely,*
> *   and one who sows discord in a family.*
> — Proverbs 6:16–19 (NRSV)

The testimony of the early church was: "Behold, how they love one another."

Healthy communication always travels upstream.

<u>Teaching 2</u>
Four More Principles Every Church Leader Should Take to Heart

1. Ministry flows from community

The biblical image for the church that I like best is Community of Disciples: "The twelve called together the whole community of the disciples" (Acts 6:2, NRSV).

Ministry is intertwined with community. Often people begin with organizing around ministry and will overlook the call to community. Henri Nouwen presents the biblical pattern for the relationship between ministry and community; it starts with solitude.

Moving from Solitude to Community to Ministry:

Now it happened in those days that Jesus went onto the mountain to pray, and he spent the whole night in prayer to God.

When day came, he summoned his disciples and picked out twelve of them and called them apostles: Simon, whom he called Peter; and his brother, Andrew; James; John; Philip; Bartholomew; Matthew; Thomas; James, son of Alphaeus; Simon, called the Zealot; Judas, son of James; and Judas Iscariot, who became a traitor.

He then came down with them and stopped at a piece of level ground where there was a large gathering of his disciples. There was a great crowd of people from all parts of Judea and Jerusalem and the coastal region of Tyre and Sidon, who had come to hear him and be cured of their diseases. And people tormented by unclean spirits were also cured. Everyone in the crowd was trying to touch him because power came out of him that cured them all. (Luke 6:12–19)

In solitude we hear the voice of the Beloved, that we are beloved. Once we have heard and received that word in the deepest parts of our soul, we become radically free. We become free from the need for someone else to meet our needs. You may disappoint me, but my soul is at rest because I am loved by my heavenly Father.

If we try to begin with ministry, I relate to you so that you will fulfill my need, namely: to accomplish ministry. Thus, I am grasping at you to meet my need. Consequently, I am not free; neither are you free. Your worth to me is based only upon your ability to meet my needs.

Community is when one person who has heard the voice of the Beloved comes into relationship with another who has heard the voice of the Beloved. They are then free on the need for the other to meet their needs.

Ministry is the overflow of community. People respond to the overflow of community. They are attracted to those whose souls are at rest because they have heard the voice of the Beloved.

• *Exercise: How much of your time do you spend with group formation? Does your vestry enjoy being together? How much do people feel cared for?*

2. The way to grow a church is not by bringing in more people but by developing stronger leaders

Here's an exercise that illustrates this principle. Consider that you rate leadership ability on a scale of one to five:

1. Attender

2. Good team member

3. Small team leader

4. Supervisor

5. Leader of leaders

Let's say you have five people that you'd like to serve as leaders of ministries.

If they are all level 1 or level 2 leaders, here's what their leadership quotient looks like:

$$1 \times 1 \times 2 \times 2 = 4$$

Thus, you have a total leadership quotient of 4.

Now, imagine that these four people have been developed as leaders, and each has grown to the next level of leadership:

$$2 \times 2 \times 3 \times 3 = 36$$

Now you have a leadership quotient of 36.

Leaders will mobilize and develop new leaders, who will grow the church.

• *Exercise: Review an area of ministry that is underperforming. Rate the leaders in that ministry on this 1 to 5 scale. What does the leadership quotient tell you about what you are trying to accomplish?*

3. Leaders will attract leaders only at their leadership level and below

That is, a level 3 leader will attract only level 1, 2, and 3 leaders, but not level 4 or 5 leaders. A level 4 leader who serves under a level 3 leader will eventually be frustrated by the level 3 leader's inability to move the group beyond a level 3.

* *Exercise: Using the same scale, check to see if the ministry that you're looking at have group members with a higher leadership quotient than the person in charge.*

4. If your past is more exciting than your future, your church is in trouble

Stewardship consultants say that the hardest kind of money for a church to raise is for debt reduction. This is because you are asking people to invest in the past. The building has been built, and the urgency is past.

People will give sacrificially when there is a clear vision that is being accomplished. But, the vision is about the future, not the past. Many people will give to museums that are clearly identified as such, but not to churches that masquerade as museums.

* *Exercise: Take a look at the documentation your church prepared the last time it searched for a rector or vicar. What was listed first: the history of the church, or the vision of the church? What does this say about what is more important to the church: its past or its future?*

Teaching 3
Thinking Like a Leader

Leaders are not smarter than the people they lead; they just think differently. Effective leaders ask questions that followers don't often ask, and they exercise a commitment that is often not expected of followers. But it all starts with thinking. Basically, leaders just think differently. When people move into leadership roles, they must learn to think differently than when they were followers.

Socrates was right when he said that an unreflected life is not worth living. But take that statement a step further: in parish ministry, an unreflected life is a recipe for disaster. As you grow in leadership, you will need to spend even more time in thinking and reflecting (and praying), not less.

So how does the leader think like a leader? There are an awful lot of leadership theories out there. It is easy to keep yourself so busy reading about leadership that you don't really have enough time to lead. Here are some starting points.

The Leader and Group Responsibility

The first change that takes place in leadership thinking is that leaders are no longer responsible only for themselves. They are now responsible for others. Whether this involves scheduling or convincing others to adopt a new idea, leaders now have to take others into consideration.

Also, it is no longer acceptable for leaders to live only in the world of their own opinions; they must be aware of the opinions and values of those whom they are leading as well. What if they don't agree? How do I influence them to change? Or am I the one who must change? As John Donne said, "No man is an island, entire unto himself." Or as John Maxwell says, "The leader who has no followers is only taking a walk."

Thus, decision-making as a leader is not based on the power to make a decision that others must submit to, but is a burden placed on the leader to consider the overall welfare of the organization as well as the concerns, maturity, and willingness of those being led in accomplishing the given task.

Leadership Is about Earning Trust

Leadership is ultimately a process of earning trust and taking (educated) risks for the well-being of the organization. Often first-time leaders view their role as simply getting to make the important decisions. However, true leadership recognizes that trust must be earned and that leaders who have earned little trust have not earned the right to make major decisions on behalf of the group or the organization. To understand the kinds of risks that a leader can take, we must understand the difference between "transactional" and "transformational" leadership.

Two Kinds of Leadership: Transactional Leadership and Transformational Leadership

James MacGregor Burns in his book *Leadership* (Harper & Row, 1978) makes a distinction between what he calls "transactional" leadership and "transformational" leadership.

Transactional leadership involves the task of getting things done. Followers will follow the leader because there is something in it for the followers. A transactional leader will encourage with statements such as:

- "Sell so many widgets and you'll make so much money."
- "If you will do this and this, you will be a success."

Transformational leadership has a moral dimension to it. It involves the leader tuning into the perceived motives of the followers and inviting them to follow based upon higher motives and morality. Transformational leadership involves such things as vision, integrity, ideals, and values. A transformational leader will encourage with statements such as:

- "I know it's difficult, but it's the right thing to do."
- "Faith is the substance of things hoped for, the evidence of things not seen."

Two things are important to know about transactional leadership:

1. It comprises the vast majority of exchanges between leaders and followers. This kind of leadership is based upon mutual reward for both leader and follower.

2. Transactional leadership is the lower form of leadership. It has no real moral dimension or sense of intrinsic right and wrong. It accepts the goals, structure, values, and culture of the existing organization. Transactional leadership works within the existing system to accomplish the goals of the organization.

The aim of transformational leadership is to influence major changes in the organization and build commitment for the long haul. Greater commitment among followers is fostered by means of commitment to shared values. Instead of accepting the status quo of the organization, through transformational leadership the leader aims to lead the organization to a preferred future, a higher level.

The leader must first be an effective transactional leader, accomplishing those transactional tasks and achieving certain successes in setting the group on task, sort of "getting the trains to run on time." When leaders have shown they can accomplish those lower level tasks, they then earn the right to lead the organization to a higher level, the transformational level, the level of vision, values, and meaning. In fact, if the leader remains at the transactional level and never moves to the transformational level, the congregation will plateau and will eventually — sooner rather than later — fall into decline.

Four Essential Components of Leadership Thinking

The leader's task is really fairly simple: to solve problems in the organization. As we showed in the last section, the leader starts at the lower, transactional, level of leadership and then moves to the higher, transformational, level. The aim is to lead the congregation and individuals within the congregation to a higher level. That's what I mean when I say that the leader's task is to solve problems. Some problems will be lower-level challenges, and some will be higher-level challenges.

Regardless of which level you are dealing with, leadership thinking has four different components:

1. Define the current reality. In *Leadership Is an Art* (Dell, 1989), Max DePree says that the first task of leadership is to define reality. (By the way, the last task is to say, "Thank you." Don't forget to say it.) So you have to ask yourself and others, "What is happening?" Your ability to articulate the reality of the current situation will affect not only the solutions you come up with, but people's willingness to follow you as well. If you paint a picture of current reality that doesn't make sense to them, they will follow you no further. Thus, it is important that you define currently reality in such a way that makes sense to your followers.

2. Account for what is happening. Or, how did we get here? Louis Leakey, the noted anthropologist, said, "The past is the key to our future." It is important to know the background of the organization, ministry, or program that you are dealing with. Knowing the seminal stories of the organization and being able to tell the stories will help people to understand both how they got to that place as well as their place in the greater ongoing history of the congregation. Placing them within the context of the salvation history of the church gives their individual role dignity, meaning, and significance.

3. Knowing where the organization is headed. It's not always so important to know exactly what the end result will be. Sometimes God wants to do something even bigger or different than we ever imagined.

The important thing is to give people hope and confidence in God's desired future. You may not know the exact destination, but you can be confident in the direction. In our home we have a framed calligraphy of a quote attributed to Martin Luther:

> This life therefore is not righteousness
> but growth in righteousness
> not health but healing,
> not being but becoming
> not rest but exercise.
> We are not yet what we shall be
> but we are growing toward it,
> the process is not yet finished
> but it is going on,
> this is not the end
> but it is the road.
> All does not yet gleam in glory
> but all is being purified.

I once asked a friend if he had any leaders on his vestry. He said, "No, but I have a lot of characters." If you don't have a sense of direction in which to lead the congregation, the "characters" among you will set the agenda every time. If you don't know where the church is headed, it will probably go in the direction of the loudest voice.

4. Make plans...and hold people accountable...and bless the people. Finally, make plans based on the first three components. How will you remedy the situation? Many people are very good at identifying the problem. The day will be won by the leader who can determine the course of action that will bring about the desired outcomes. However, making plans is not enough. The leader must keep people on task by holding them accountable. Finally, bless the people and celebrate their successes.

Questions for Discussion

1. *Who have been the three most influential people in your life? Why were they significant to you? How did they motivate you, through coercion or encouragement? How did you feel when it was all over?*

2. *Reflect on the responsibilities you have in setting people to task. Why should they want to follow you? What preferred future are you offering them? What's in it for them?*

3. *If you were to leave your position today with absolutely no forewarning, how would the person that follows you begin to take over your responsibilities? Would she have to start from scratch? Would she have to have someone explain to her exactly what to do? How would she know what her responsibilities are and what you intended for the group to accomplish this year?*

4. *How many thank-you notes have you written to those you are leading? Do people view you as appreciative of their hard work or presumptuous in your attitude toward them?*

Teaching 4
Congregational Development According to Yogi

It's that time of year. Baseball. The trees regain their leaves. The weather turns warm. And baseball fans look forward in eager anticipation to "America's Favorite Pastime."

In anticipation of this time of year, let's turn to that great twentieth-century theologian Yogi Berra for some wisdom on congregational development. So put on your batting helmet and let's go.

1. *We have a good time together, even when we're not together*. Yogi said this about his wife, Carmen. This speaks to community. Vision is what unites the disparate activities of a congregation. Mission is the focus of what we're about. When we're living into a common vision, even when we're not together we have a good time together.

2. *The future ain't what it used to be*. Yogi says that, even though times change, you should never compromise your values. God's faithfulness remains true. The apostolic tradition, of which we are heirs, remains ours. Methods change. God doesn't. We should remain steadfast in essentials but charitable in the non-essentials.

3. *If you don't know where you're going, you might not get there*. Yogi says that he focused early in his life on baseball. If the best days of your church's life are in the past, your church is in trouble. Hebrews 11:1 tells us that "faith is the substance of things hoped for, the evidence of things not seen." Unless we have a picture in our mind of a better future, there is no reason to have faith or to ask people to stretch beyond themselves.

4. *You can observe a lot by watching*. Yogi was asked to be the manager of the New York Yankees in 1963 by Ralph Houk, who was then both manager and general manager. Ralph would manage for the 1963 season and Yogi would watch for the whole year. Then, in 1964, when to everyone's surprise Yogi Berra was named manager of the New York Yankees, he knew he was ready to manage because he had been watching Ralph Houk and others manage for a whole year, knowing that he would be in their shoes the next year. We can all learn from someone else — if we watch.

5. *It gets late early out here*. Yogi was talking about playing left field and how much sooner the setting sun got in his eyes in some ball fields. This is true for churches as well. Many times a church will

import a program that was successful in another church without considering the implications of that program for the people they are actually serving. What worked in one place may need some adapting to make it work in your place.

6. *Question: What time is it? Answer (Yogi): Do you mean now?* Look around you. If a Martian were to come to your church, what year would that alien think that it is? What do your Sunday school materials, office materials, communications, furniture and furnishings say that the year is? Are you using methods that would appeal to the 1950s or the 2000s?

7. *We have deep depth.* Often ministries are one key person away from extinction. Healthy ministries and healthy leaders have a leader (apprentice) in the wings who can take over if the leader were to leave or become incapacitated in some way. If that leader cannot reproduce himself or herself, then chances are that that ministry is not key to the mission of the church, or it does not really tap into the core values of the church, or the leader is not really an effective leader. It may be the leader's desire for that ministry to be continued, but it's not really a value held by the church.

8. And, of course, *It ain't over until it's over.* We learn two things from Yogi on this matter. First, don't give up. Sometimes people need permission to say "No" twice before they can say "Yes" once. Failure is not final. Just because we did something like this once doesn't mean we're going to do it the same way the second time. We may, in fact, succeed the second time because we tweaked one or two things, or maybe the timing was just right.

9. The other thing we learn from Yogi is that sometimes *It's over.* Yogi tells about being fired by a subordinate of George Steinbrenner and staying away from Yankee Stadium for fourteen years. Finally, Steinbrenner came and apologized to Yogi. Yogi forgave him. He said, "Fourteen years is a long time to hold a grudge. It's over." There may be a grudge in your life that you need to let go of — whether in your family, your individual life, or your church. Broken relationships do tremendous damage to the body

of Christ. Remember the bumper sticker that says, "Christians aren't perfect . . . just forgiven."

Teaching 5
Introduction to Congregational Size Dynamics

To the Leader: When presenting the material on Congregational Size Dynamics, it is best to present the material on the size of your church at present, the next smaller size (if applicable), as well as the next size you want to grow to. This gives your leaders a sense of the present, the past, and the desired future.

Congregational Size Dynamics is a shorthand attempt to understand the interrelationships between the congregational leadership and the congregation. It is based on the premise that groups of people gathered around a common purpose relate to leadership and to one another within the group in fairly consistent and, actually, predictable ways.

According to this way of looking at the local church, a small Episcopal church has more in common — in terms of how its members relate to one another and its leadership — with a Baptist or a Methodist church of a similar size than with a large Episcopal church. Thus, to be effective, leadership needs to take into account the dynamics peculiar to the size and prepare the greater complexity of the next larger size.

Overview of Sizes

Congregational Size Dynamics groups churches according to their average Sunday attendance (ASA). Experience has shown this to be a more useful indicator than membership. The original work on this was done by Arlin Rothauge and his categories were revised by Kevin Martin.

Each size but one relates to itself comfortably. That is to say, each size has a "natural" way of being the church. When a church at each size is functioning well, most of the people are generally unconcerned with the processes of how the church operates. The structure of the church is not an issue. However, in one of these sizes below, as well as when the church is transitioning between sizes, the organization of the church becomes more of an issue for its leaders. When a church is in the transitional zone between sizes, it is more difficult to move the church from one size to another.

We group churches into five size categories:

Category	ASA
Family	3–75
Pastoral	76–140
Transitional	120–250
Program	225–450
Resource	451+

As we look at each size, we will highlight: the role of leadership, congregational life, and church growth. The church has unseen forces both encouraging growth to the next natural level as well as countervailing forces inhibiting growth that aim to return the church to a prior, more natural level of equilibrium.

"But this doesn't apply to my church"

Some of the suggested characteristics may not apply to your church. Remember that these church sizes provide an introduction for discussing the inner dynamics of the church. Some will be obvious in their presence while others will not be. The important thing is to begin the discussion so that people will be aware of the implications of the forces at work.

But be careful. Churches are often tempted to apply larger church characteristics to their church. This may be an indication that your church is overorganized in a way inappropriate to your natural size.

Teaching 6
The Family-sized Church

The family-sized church has an average Sunday attendance of 3 to 75. These churches are typically, but not exclusively, located in smaller towns. They function much as a family does, and the leadership of the church is often made up of a couple of extended families. Not everyone in the church is a member of the extended family, but one prominent extended family is often at the center of influence. The strength of this congregation is in its intimacy. The weakness is its low expectations. Finances are often an issue as well.

Congregational Life

The organization is a single cell. Just as in the television sitcom *Cheers,* the hallmark of this church is "everybody knows your name." Fellowship is often informal and not always at the church, because these individuals and families gather together at other places besides the church. Communications are by word of mouth. If people don't know about something until they read it in the church newsletter, they are really "out of the loop." Pastoral care is done person to person. The pastor is there for major crises, such as hospital visits, deaths, and so on, but much pastoral care is done informally among the congregation. It is better for this church to adopt one major mission or outreach project that the whole church can identify with and rally around than to try to do too much or simply to spread its limited financial resources around.

Leadership

The ordained person in this sized church is not the real leader of the congregation (family). Instead, the ordained person functions as the chaplain to the congregation. The congregation expects primarily pastoral care from the pastor: counseling, prayers at appropriate occasions, hospital visits, weddings, funerals, and so on; but the real decisions affecting the church are made by longstanding members of the congregation.

The true leader in this congregational family system is designated as the matriarch or patriarch. This person is usually a long-term member of both the congregation and the community and will typically have siblings, children, and grandchildren in the congregation. The church is really a set of a few extended family units with a few other friends as well.

Although the vestry is the stated lay leadership circle, usually the vestry will defer to the matriarch or patriarch. It is not unusual to have a vestry make a decision only to have the same vestry reverse itself a month later after everyone has talked to the matriarch or patriarch of the congregation. Woe be unto the pastor who serves a family-sized church who really believes that she is the leader of the congregation.

This sized congregation will have approximately two to eight leaders. Effective leadership by the pastor is often done "behind the scenes," often consulting with the matriarch or patriarch. Success for this church, in the eyes of the congregation, is in keeping the doors open.

Church Growth

Church growth is carried out by introducing the newcomer to the matriarch and patriarch and having that individual or family become a part of the matriarch's or patriarch's family and friendship circle. They should be invited to the congregation's "pot-luck" dinners or simply to dinner after church at a local restaurant. The newcomer needs to feel accepted by the ongoing members.

<u>Teaching 7</u>
The Pastoral-sized Church

The pastoral-sized church has an average Sunday attendance of 76 to 140. The first thing one notices is that the leadership has shifted from the matriarch or patriarch to the pastor. These churches are still single cell in nature. Although not everyone knows everyone else's name, they all recognize each other and will also notice if someone is new to the congregation.

People are attracted to this church because of the intimacy among the congregation. A person can miss church one Sunday, return the next, and five different people will ask what they have been doing or how their trip was. A church of this size can give to its members a real sense of belonging and family.

Congregational Life

Church life in the pastoral-sized church is highly relational. Rather than being program-centered like the program-sized and resource-sized churches, people are a part of the pastoral-sized church primarily through its worship service and the web of interrelationships within the congregation.

The strength of this congregation is in its stability. When this sized church is functioning well, it is a delight to be a part of. People feel cared for; they know others by name and are noticed when they miss church. Assuming that the physical property of the church is in good repair, this church can sustain itself for a long time. Worship services are provided on a regular basis, and the parishioners generally know what to expect in them. Individuals can rise in leadership and responsibility. Each member expects, and can usually get, equal access to the pastor. The pastor is always available for counseling as well as for more personal social occasions.

The weakness of this congregation is in its predictability. The programs offered by this congregation are generic and small. Don't expect a very large choir and don't expect the choir to sing very challenging music. The youth group is often no larger than a Bible study. Planning for this church is usually based on "what did we do last year?" This year's budget looks suspiciously like last year's, and the year before that, and the year before that. Often leaders are tired, because there are more leadership positions than there are emerging leaders, so people are often weary from having too many church responsibilities.

Because this is such a comfortable church to be in, it can be easy to become ingrown. Therefore, this sized church should have an identifiable mission and outreach project that unites the congregation. But it should also limit its missions and outreach endeavors to what the members actually participate in. Additionally, there will be larger churches in the surrounding area that are engaged in activities with which this church can't compete. So what it does, it should do with excellence. A good word to this congregation's is Mother Teresa's counsel: "Do small things well." And take care of relationships.

Leadership

This church is more clergy-centered than the family-sized church. The role of the ordained person can be described as the *paterfamilias*. That is, instead of functioning primarily as the chaplain in the congregation, this ordained person is the focal point of all activities.

This pastor is, indeed, the leader of the congregation. The pastor in this sized church is usually expected to give her opinion on flower arrangements and paint colors, to assign the setting up of chairs, to pray before parish gatherings, to be the first to the hospital, and so on. The pastoral-sized church pastor is the primary evangelist in the congregation as well. She will be the primary drawing card in bringing new people into the congregation.

This sized congregation will have approximately eight to twenty-five leaders. It is tempting for this church to want to organize itself as a larger church would. Often these churches are overorganized for their size, requiring their leaders to handle too many tasks.

The role of the vestry at this level is to serve as the unpaid staff of the church. Because a church of this size generally has only one full-time staff member, namely, the pastor, the vestry members are often the ones who carry out the plans of the rector and the congregation. When the vestry of the pastoral-sized church sees itself as simply decision makers for the congregation, the pastor becomes overworked, and the church is not set up for the appropriate and healthy transition to a larger size.

Church Growth

The pastor has the primary responsibility of incorporating newcomers into the ongoing life of the church. The key to making newcomers feel like they belong is for them to have a relationship with the pastor. In this sized church, the pastor is the glue that holds everyone together — both newcomers and longtime members. Really, growth depends on the energy of the pastor and on the church's ability to provide the basic ministries that are expected of churches: worship, pastoral care, missions and outreach, and Christian formation.

Because the pastor is the primary evangelist and person who incorporates people into the life of the church, there is a danger for people who only come to worship who have not made friends among the congregation. When the pastor leaves, it is easy for these folks to fall away from the church and wait to see whether they like the next pastor. For the church to grow beyond the pastoral church size, it must pay attention to incorporating its members into ministries beyond the Sunday worship service.

One other word of caution: pastoral-sized church pastors often yield to the temptation of trying one new program after another without really following through. Parishioners get weary of trying one new program after another. Plan for the long term on new ministries. Plan for success, not just to try a new program to see how people respond.

Teaching 8
The Transitional-sized Church

The transitional-sized church, generally having an average Sunday attendance of 120 to 250, is not a natural size. Pastoral-sized churches are a natural size, and program-sized churches are a natural size. When these churches are functioning well, the size of the church is not really an issue in the congregation's life. This is not true for transitional-sized churches. Designating a church as "transitional-sized" is another way of saying that it is a sort of hybrid church: it is not pastoral-sized, and it is not program-sized. Churches of the other sizes usually function in a state of equilibrium. There is never really a state of equilibrium in the transitional-sized church.

In this sized church the smaller and the larger church sizes compete for supremacy. In the smaller church with an average Sunday attendance of 3 to 150, there is internal pressure to preserve intimacy. As the church begins to grow, somewhere around an average Sunday attendance of 120 to 180, there is an external pressure to provide quality programming.

The transitional-sized church is like an adolescent boy who is going through a growth spurt. His voice is changing; his clothes don't fit; he feels awkward and gangly. Just as it takes patience to help the adolescent through this challenging time in his life, it also takes patience to help the transitional-sized church through this awkward time in its life. The difference is that the adolescent *will* become a teenager; without proper guidance and appropriate changes at various levels, the transitional-sized church will *not* make it through to a program size.

Congregational Life

Kevin Martin, dean of St. Matthew's Cathedral in Dallas, Texas, says that the transitional-sized church is 75 percent pastoral and 75 percent program. What he means is that, at any given time, 75 percent of the congregation is expecting the church to function as a pastoral-sized church, and 75 percent of the congregation is expecting the church to function as a program-sized church — all at the same time! (Yes, 75 plus 75 does not add up to 100. It's like the "Pushmi-pullyu" of Dr. Doolittle fame.) That is the challenge of the transitional-sized church. In fact, some church members have their own self-contradictory expectations for the church, wanting it to be both small and intimate while at the same time offering the quality programs characteristic of a larger church.

Some programs in this church are well developed while others are underdeveloped. There is a growing number of people demanding an expanding number of specialized ministries but often not enough of these folks to comprise a critical mass that will sufficiently populate and provide leadership for these specialized ministries.

Leadership

The role of the pastor in the transitional-sized church is threefold: non-anxious presence, vision caster, and developer of leaders. Because of these competing and contradictory expectations, this is the most-stressed congregation and the most-stressed pastor. The effective pastor must therefore be a non-anxious presence, because almost everyone else is anxious. The congregation has both rising expectations for future growth as well as fear of the loss of intimacy from no longer being a smaller congregation.

One of the ways of being a non-anxious presence is for the pastor to be an effective vision-caster. What the wise pastor knows is that as the church grows a little larger, there is light at the end of the tunnel — and it is not an oncoming train. Experience with other transitional-to program-sized churches shows that something amazing happens when the church grows upward to an average Sunday attendance of 225 to 250. As it moves out of transitional size and into the program size, things begin to "settle down" emotionally for the congregation. An almost palpable feeling of calm begins to pervade the congregation. At this larger size, although the congregation is just as busy as it was at the smaller size, the healthy stability of predictability and confidence begins to pervade the congregation. Vision will empower people to stretch and sacrifice through the anxiety-laden transitional size to that 225 to 250 period of increased stability. Pastors who do not make this transition themselves in their vision-casting and management ability among the congregation eventually "grow the church down" to their own comfort level.

The third role of the pastor is to be a developer of leaders. She must develop leaders because a church of this size is characterized by a number of programs that "haven't yet arrived." The transitional-sized church has lots of needs and interests but not always that critical mass necessary to have a fully functioning ministry in individual areas. It never has enough leaders. In fact, the best description for this sized church is the Madeleine Kahn character, Lili Von Schtupp, in the movie *Blazing Saddles,* who sings, "I'm tired." So many lay leaders are tired in the transitional-sized church because there are not enough leaders to fill all the roles for the jobs that need to be done. It is critical for the growth of the church that the pastor transition from being the primary provider of ministry to being the developer of leaders.

The vestry is also transitioning, from the unpaid staff of the church to the vision-casting, policy-enabling board that fosters the growth that is both natural and unnatural to this church. This church must become a staff-run church. If the vestry does not transition to accommodate this more complex entity, the internal pressure to preserve intimacy will overpower the external pressure to provide quality programming. There are many, many churches that had their potential for growth cut short because either the pastor or the vestry failed to make the transition to a more complex way of being the church.

Church Growth

Church growth is accomplished at this level by paying attention to the small things: adding a ministry here; improving a ministry there; adding a part-time staff member to reach new people; providing resources for a ministry to help it move to a higher level of excellence; cleaning, fixing, and painting; crisper communications media.

It is easy for people to begin to feel lost as this church grows to a more complex size. The incorporation of newcomers becomes important as the church shifts from an informal, oral culture to a more programmed approach. Priority should be placed on recruiting either a volunteer or part-time person to oversee the incorporation of newcomers, helping them to join in a ministry or small group within the church. Healthy growth requires that the church shift from a pastor-focused process of incorporation to a lay-led, program-based process of incorporation.

In addition, look for some people to complain about various concerns in the congregation as these changes occur. Often those complaints are really "ricochets," masking their underlying concerns. That is, the real concern for some of these parishioners will be the changes that are occuring, but they won't complain about those changes. Rather, they will complain that "the pastor has changed." "This isn't the same church that I joined," and so on. The underlying concern is based on the changes among the congregation. However, the concerns articulated will have little or nothing to do with those changes.

Further attention needs to be given to expanding missions and outreach involvement but without overburdening already overworked leaders. Churches of this size need programs, people, resources, and buildings all at once. Thus, the leadership should be thoughtfully and prayerfully strategic in what it adds. Further, it should make sure that it provides the necessary support and follow-through for new ministries and programs.

Teaching 9
The Program-sized Church

The program-sized church has an average Sunday attendance of 225 to 450 (note the overlap in size). Whereas the spiritual nourishment in a pastoral-sized church occurs primarily through a relationship with the pastor, in the program-sized church most spiritual nourishment takes place though the programs of the church — supplemented by the pastor. This church is characterized by the presence of activity and program offerings. There is a place to land for just about everyone in a church of this size.

The typical parishioner in a program-sized church knows the same number of people as the typical parishioner in a pastoral-sized church; however, there are simply more people for the parishioner in the program-sized church not to know. The quality of relationships is no less significant or meaningful, although it may seem so to the average pastoral-sized church member. One often hears people in a pastoral-sized church say, "We don't want to become like one of those mega-churches."

The strength of this church is in its program offerings. Senior pastors can come and go; as long as they don't do significant damage to the congregation, the programs will carry this congregation along. Most of the staff are trained and paid fairly and generally carry out their responsibilities quite well. People, particularly in suburban areas, are attracted to program-sized churches because they have programs that will meet most needs and interests of youth, children, men, women, choir, and so on.

Congregational Life

Congregational life is lived through subgroupings of people. Ministries are generally run well in this size of church. Staff is often capable, and people who are comfortable in a larger church are often very satisfied with the quality and range of programming.

Leadership

The leadership role of the pastor is the most difficult shift for churches and clergy moving from a transitional-to a program-sized church. Whereas in the pastoral-sized church, the pastor does a lot of hands-on ministry among members, the program-sized pastor pastors primarily the leaders of the congregation, with leadership development, vision, and administration taking the greatest share of the pastor's time.

The pastor is still at the center of the life of the congregation, but his role has shifted. Newcomers in a program-sized church don't expect to know the senior pastor on a personal basis. They may be in church five times before exchanging more than twenty-five words with the pastor. Likewise, parishioners don't usually expect a hospital visit from the senior pastor; although it *is* expected in a time of crisis or real need. The senior pastor spends his time planning with other staff members and lay leaders in the congregation, recruiting new leaders, facilitating the activities in the congregation, and keeping the programs running smoothly.

Clergypersons who derive their primary satisfaction in parish ministry from performing direct, hands-on pastoral care will be very dissatisfied in a church of this size. Most pastoral ministry is lay-led, because the ordained persons spend so much of their time mobilizing lay leaders. They must have most of their ministry needs satisfied through their work with staff and other leaders. If they spend too much time in pastoral care, the leaders will go uncared for and will not be properly supervised and developed.

Similarly, the vestry of a church of this size serves as the vision-casting, vision-bearing, vision-communicating, and policy-forming leadership group of the church. With the senior pastor, they grasp the vision of the church and keep it on course in fulfilling the vision. The day-to-day operations of the church are directed by the staff.

It is a challenge for people who have served on the vestry of a smaller church to adjust to leadership of a larger, program-sized church. They tend to look at the church through smaller eyes and want to be involved in the day-to-day management operations of the church as was their practice in the smaller church.

Church Growth

Incorporation of newcomers is accomplished through this church's programs. The assimilation process is based on a programmatic offering. Classes and get-togethers are offered on a regular basis; compare this to the pastoral-sized church's approach to newcomers' classes: "Whenever we have enough newcomers to need a class." A church of this size has many side doors into the congregation, such as Mothers' Day Out, the choir, Bible studies, youth ministries, and so on.

Teaching 10
The Resource-sized Church

We turn now to the largest size under consideration: the resource-sized church, with an average Sunday attendance of 451 plus. The hallmark of this size church is excellence. The facilities are top-notch, the music is well done; the nursery is clean and neat and staffed by well-trained personnel; the printed materials are all attractive. Everything is done with excellence, and members of the congregation expect this.

Congregational Life

This church has a large, professional staff. There is much room for advancement for lay leaders. In fact, the resource-sized church will often hire lay leaders from within the congregation for new staff positions. They are the ones who are most conversant with and supportive of the vision of the congregation. Further, this church is noted for its specialized programs offered to smaller and more discrete subgroups within the culture.

This church is usually not simply one congregation but is made up of smaller congregations within the larger church. It may have a small group structure or some other way to break down the congregation into more identifiable and socially cohesive subgroups. Parishioners will give up a close relationship with the senior pastor in favor of the quality programs and ministries offered by the resource-sized church.

Leadership

The senior pastor is like the president of a university, managing several "deans" as well as a large staff of a very complex and diverse congregation. He must be able to articulate the unique vision of the church and keep a large staff on task and living into the vision of the congregation. The effective senior pastor, then, is a motivator and vision-bearer and communicator, a symbol of unity, stability, and energy for the congregation.

The vestry functions in a fashion similar to that of the program-sized church, affirming the vision of the church and giving permission for new non-generic ministries to be started. (Non-generic ministries are those ministries beyond the basics of Sunday school, choir, altar guild, and so on found in the vast majority of transitional and smaller-sized churches.) In a resource-sized church, the vestry must focus its resources on the ever-expanding mission of the church. If the mission doesn't expand, the church will begin to plateau, and decline will soon follow. Because of its size, the number of worship services (sub-congregations) and the general stability of its financial base, decline in this church is often imperceptible by the vast majority of its parishioners until a crisis of some sort makes the (previously unnoticed) decline an issue.

Church Growth

Likewise, newcomers are drawn to the resource-sized church because of its program offerings. The non-generic ministries of resource-sized churches bring in new people that smaller churches will not attract. Often these larger churches provide a safety valve or way station for exiles from smaller congregations in conflict or will attract people from smaller congregations that do not provide the quality programs, for example, youth ministry, that they are looking for.

Incorporation becomes very important in a church this large. It is easy for people to "fall through the cracks," particularly as some are attracted to this church because they can initially be invisible for awhile. If they remain invisible for too long, they will similarly drift away.

Teaching 11
Why Organizations Fail*

Error #1: Allowing too much complacency.

In Other Words: Establish a sense of urgency.

- *Identify crises, potential crises, or major opportunities that can create urgency.*

- *Balance between "gloom and doom" and "we're doing just great."*

Error #2: Failing to create a sufficiently powerful guiding coalition.

In Other Words: Create a team that works together.

- *Identify and establish a group with enough influence, confidence, capability, and expertise to lead the change effort, inspire trust, and function well as a team.*

- *Distinguish between "characters" and "leaders."*

Error #3: Underestimating the power of vision.

In Other Words: Develop a strong and compelling vision.

- *Do you have a vision that people will sacrifice for?*

- *Vision unites, plans divide.*

Elements of a Vision

- Provides a future picture of the organization
- Appeals to long-term interests of stakeholders
- Is clear enough to guide decision-making
- Is general enough to permit individual initiative
- is easy to communicate

---

*From John P. Kotter, *Leading Change* (Boston: Harvard Business School Press, 1996).

Error #4: Undercommunicating the vision by a factor of 10 (or 100 or even 1,000).

In Other Words: Communicate the vision of change.

* *Use every method possible to communicate — continually.*

* *Leadership must model the expected behavior.*

Vision Communications Principles

* Use metaphors, analogies, and examples
* Tell stories
* Use different forums to communicate vision
* Lead by example
* Listen and be listened to
* Address seeming inconsistencies between vision and actions
* Repeat, repeat, repeat

Error #5: Permitting obstacles to derail the new vision.

In Other Words: Empower positive action.

* *Empower people to implement the vision by removing obstacles to its implementation.*

Error #6: Failing to create short-term wins.

In Other Words: Start with short-term wins before you attempt bigger risks.

* *Plan specifically to create visible improvements or wins within six to eighteen months of launch.*

* *Provide public recognition and rewards to those who have participated in the wins.*

Empowerment Principles

- Restructure whenever necessary to remove structural barriers
- Provide skills training necessary to implement the vision
- Align performance evaluation, compensation decisions, promotions, and recruiting and hiring systems
- Encourage risk-taking and non-traditional ideas, activities, and actions
- Confront those in authority who undercut the change that is needed

---

Error #7: Declaring victory too soon.

In Other Words: Consolidate change and produce more change.

- *Use the increased credibility derived from earlier changes to drive deeper change.*

Error #8: Neglecting to anchor change in the corporate culture.

In Other Words: These changes mustn't be based simply on the leader's personality.

- *Anchor change (new goals, attitudes, behavior) in the culture of the organization (i.e., its social norms and shared values).*

Consequences of Failing to Lead Healthy Change

- New strategies aren't implemented well.
- Acquisitions don't achieve expected synergies.
- Reengineering takes too long and costs too much.
- Downsizing doesn't get costs under control.
- Quality programs don't deliver hoped-for results.

Twelve

Mental Exercises

O God, because without you we are not able to please you, mercifully grant that your Holy Spirit may in all things direct and rule our hearts; through Jesus Christ our Lord, who lives and reigns with you and the Holy Spirit, one God, now and for ever. Amen.

The mental exercises that follow will require your vestry to put on their congregational consultants' hats. The exercises are designed not to give your leaders answers but to help them ask the right questions — and then to challenge them to answer those questions. They will allow vestry members to look at their church with fresh eyes and to notice things that they might previously have overlooked.

The Icebreaker Questions are designed to help the vestry members to get to know each other and possibly learn things about each other that they might not have known. Most of the other Mental Exercises will help the vestry reflect on different aspects of the church in such a way as to suggest positive changes that the vestry can propose that may bring fairly immediate improvements to the church. Using these exercises periodically will provide a change of pace for the vestry meeting. On the other hand, engaging in these kinds of exercises several months in a row may result in change overload and tire the vestry out as they address all the changes that need to be made.

Mental Exercise 1
How to Spend Your Summer Vacation

How often do pastors get impatient with and try to devise various ways to combat the "summer slump," where so many people are absent from church? Here's an exercise for the congregation that will take advantage of people's summer vacations.

At the beginning of the summer before people leave for vacation, encourage them to visit the local church — Episcopal or otherwise — where they are vacationing, bring back their Sunday worship leaflet, and write down one or two things that they liked about the church they visited.

Then, around August 1, have a parish-wide "Summer Show and Tell" at which people can share their summer experiences at other churches, for example, how they were welcomed, how they were made to feel as newcomers, and what they liked about the churches they visited. Be sure to have someone from the vestry or church staff take notes.

Post the worship leaflets on a bulletin board in the parish hall to let people see what sorts of churches have been visited and how these churches present their worship and communicate their announcements on Sundays.

Mental Exercise 2
General Introduction Icebreaker Question – 1

Please give your name, how long you've been at St. John's, what drew you to St. John's, and what keeps you at St. John's.

Explanation: When people recount the story of their coming to the church, we often see that the pattern of their relationship with their former church repeats itself in their new church. If they came from a conflicted church situation, they likely will display conflicted relationships at St. John's. Similarly, if they served in leadership at a smaller or larger church, they will likely relate to St. John's as a smaller or larger church, respectively. Also, this can be a time of affirming positive characteristics that drew people to the church.

Mental Exercise 3
General Introduction Icebreaker Question – 2

Please complete the following sentence: The spiritual gift, talent, skill, ability, experience, or perspective that I bring to this vestry is....

Explanation: Often people will serve on a vestry with no clear purpose in mind of why they are there. If we believe that God calls individuals to serve on the vestry, then it is logical to assume that God has a purpose for calling those individuals to serve. This exercise will help the group to reflect on the various gifts that people bring and explore what God might be wanting to do among and through the vestry for the coming year. Sometimes people are a bit uncomfortable talking about their gifts and abilities, but this exercise will foster deeper, more intimate sharing.

Mental Exercise 4
Is St. Swithin's a Five-Star Church?

If St. Swithin's were a restaurant, how many stars would we be rated in the following service areas?

★=Poor   ★★=Needs Improvement   ★★★=Okay
★★★★=Good   ★★★★★=Excellent

Appearance	Greeting
Parking	Music
Ushers	Sermon
Atmosphere	Childcare

1. Who are the customers for our church?

2. What are the real and felt needs of these folks?

3. What are we doing really well?

4. What are we doing poorly?

5. Whom among our target population are we not connecting with? Why?

Mental Exercise 5
Ministry Planning Exercise

For this exercise you will need:

- a poster board or fiber board to post planning notes on
- Post-it notes
- Markers

1. List all ministries currently active in the church.
2. Identify four to six ministries essential to the life of the church.
3. List the one ministry that you are passionate about that feels "pinched" right now.

Break into two or three planning groups around two or three ministries.

4. Describe what this ministry should look like at some point in the future, e.g., six months, twelve months, two years, if it were functioning as you think it ought (preferred future).
5. Describe what this ministry looks like now (current reality).
6. Using Post-it notes, identify all steps, milestones, and activities that must be completed to turn the current reality into the preferred future. Don't worry that you might get them out of order. The important thing is to come up with all the necessary elements.
7. Arrange these notes according to an appropriate chronology. This is your implementation action plan for this area of ministry.
8. Transfer this information to the Ministry Planning Sheet on the following page and complete the unanswered questions.

Good Shepherd Episcopal Church
Date:

_____

MINISTRY PLANNING SHEET

_____

Name of ministry:
Leader:
Planning team members:

Why is this ministry essential?

Describe what this ministry looks like now:

Describe what this ministry should look like at some point in the future:

What steps and actions (training, fund allocation, organization, advertising, and so on) are required to get from the present reality to the preferred future?

Person responsible for
carrying out this ministry:

Cost:

Mental Exercise 6
Mystery Worshipper

Ship of Fools, a Christian humor website (*www.ship-of-fools.com*), has a section called "Mystery Worshipper" where their volunteer "correspondents" will visit a church and rate the worship service according to friendliness, quality of sermon, music, and so on. Visit a church that is a little larger than yours and compare and contrast your church with theirs in the following areas:

* Street appeal
* Parking
* Cleanliness
* Nursery
* Restrooms
* Friendliness of ushers, greeters
* Worship bulletin
* Music
* Sermon
* Announcements
* Manner of welcoming visitors
* Emotional satisfaction of the worship service

Mental Exercise 7
Signs of the Times

Have you noticed the signs around your church lately? Have you *really* looked at them? One objection to adequate signage around the church is that "it destroys the beauty of our grounds. Besides, *everyone* knows where we are." Well, not everyone. Not the typical visitor to your church. At the heart of the matter regarding signs is the question, "Whom are we trying to reach?" If we are primarily concerned for those who are already a part of the church, then signs are unnecessary. If we are primarily concerned for the newcomer and to lessen the "unknowns" for the newcomer, then we will make sure that our signs are attractive, legible, and helpful.

My wife and I recently visited a church where we opened two doors before we found the door leading to the sanctuary. This church had parking for guests but no signs telling us where the sanctuary was. It was behind "Door Number Three." As seasoned churchgoers, we were a little embarrassed when we walked in on the choir warming up for the service. Here are a few principles to consider:

Outdoor Signs

1. Can people find you? Many of our churches are tucked away in neighborhoods. Do you have adequate "The Episcopal Church Welcomes You" signs at the major street corners near your church?

2. Is your major church sign attractive and accurate. Are the letters large enough to be seen by someone driving by at the posted speed limit? Church sign companies can provide you with specifications for how high the letters should be based upon the average driving speeds.

3. Which direction does your major church sign face? It should generally be perpendicular to the street (for drive-by traffic) rather than parallel (for walking traffic).

4. Do you have parking reserved for Visitors ("Guests") and are their signs clearly marked? Visitors often arrive immediately prior to the Sunday service after all the "good parking spaces" are gone.

5. Where is your entrance? Is it obvious to the newcomer? Where is the church office?

6. Is your facility large enough to warrant a map? At shopping malls, Six Flags, and Disneyland, "You Are Here" signs are always helpful and appreciated.

Indoor Signs

1. Where is the sanctuary? nursery? office? restroom? Sunday school?

2. Does your church have multiple entrances? Are they clearly marked?

3. Are Sunday school rooms clearly marked? You might consider posting the teacher's name along with a photo.

4. What is the sequence to your room numbers? Is the progression obvious?

While signs will not in and of themselves bring anyone into our churches, the lack of signs can create stumbling blocks that will unintentionally signal to people that they are not welcome.

Mental Exercise 8
Change Readiness Test

Are you ready for change? Or are you more interested in preserving the status quo? Is the leadership of your congregation, both staff and volunteer, ready to lead change? Please respond to the following statements by identifying your relative personal agreement on a scale of 1 to 5. Total the individual answers for each question and divide by the number of members in the group. Then compare your attitudes with those of the group as a whole.

I Totally Agree — 1 — 2 — 3 — 4 — 5 — No Way!

1. The nursery should be extra clean, neat, and staffed with paid help, and open every time there is a church function.
   Me ＿＿＿   The Group ＿＿＿

2. We should be more concerned for the feelings of our staff and volunteers than for what kind of job they are doing.
   Me ＿＿＿   The Group ＿＿＿

3. I am willing for the facilities to be used even if they get dirty.
   Me ＿＿＿   The Group ＿＿＿

4. Reaching out to new members is just as important as taking care of the present members.
   Me ＿＿＿   The Group ＿＿＿

5. I really want the church to remain the way it was when I joined.
   Me ＿＿＿   The Group ＿＿＿

6. I am seldom concerned about procedure.

   Me _____   The Group _____

7. It is important for us to pay off all previous debt before we take on new debt.

   Me _____   The Group _____

8. We may need to stretch a bit financially in order to hire new staff members.

   Me _____   The Group _____

9. Several worship services are fine with me because I am more interested in meeting the needs of all the people than I am in knowing everyone at church.

   Me _____   The Group _____

10. I am not offended when the rector (vicar) does not give me regular personal attention.

    Me _____   The Group _____

11. I believe that more staff is needed today than in the past.

    Me _____   The Group _____

12. I trust and affirm my rector's (vicar's) efforts to bring newcomers into the church.

    Me _____   The Group _____

Mental Exercise 9
The Timeline of My Life

Directions: Using the following line as a timeline of your life, sub-divide it into the major seasons of your life, such as: childhood, junior high, senior high, college, marriage, and so on. Chart the emotional highs and lows. With a different colored pen mark the spiritual highs and lows. When were you closest to God? When did you feel farthest from God? When was a time that your character was put to the test? How did you do? Share your timeline with the group.

Mental Exercise 10
What Do These Numbers Mean?

Before the vestry board can make any plans, it must have a firm grasp on current reality. Although congregational statistics don't tell the full story of a congregation's life and condition, they will reveal general trends about a congregation's general health and direction.

On a graph, plot for the past ten years the following numbers:

- average Sunday attendance

- membership

- number of pledges

- amount of pledges

- operating income

(Be sure to put these all in one graph so you can see the overall trends.)

Here are three questions for the vestry to discuss as it reflects on these numbers:

1. Define the current reality. Max DePree has said that the first task of leadership is to define reality. So you have to ask yourself and others, "What is happening?" Your ability to articulate the reality of the current situation will affect not only the solutions you come up with, but people's willingness to follow you as well. If you paint a picture of current reality that doesn't make sense to them, they will follow you no further. Thus, it is important that you define current reality in a way that makes sense to your followers.

2. Account for what is happening. Or, how did we get here? Louis Leakey, the noted anthropologist, said, "The past is the key to our future." It is important to know the background of the organization, ministry, or program that you are dealing with. Knowing the seminal stories of the organization and being able to tell those stories will help people to understand both how they got to that place as well as their place in the greater ongoing history of the congregation. Placing them within the context of the salvation history of the church gives their individual role dignity, meaning, and significance.

3. Where the organization is headed. If we continue on our present course, where will we likely be in five years? Most projections anticipate growth, and most projections fall short of their mark. Look at the general trend of your congregation over the past ten years. Is it generally growing, declining, plateaued? Do you expect your congregation to grow over the next five years? If so, why? If your congregation has not grown over the past five years, why do you expect it to grow now? What is different?

The longer a congregation has been at a certain level, the more difficult it is to bring about change. If the congregation is feeling positive about themselves, do the numbers demonstrate real growth, or is the congregation in a certain amount of denial?

<u>Mental Exercise 11</u>
Internally Focused or Externally Focused?

Is your church internally focused or externally focused? Try this exercise: list all the ministries of the church. In a second column list the number of people in the church reached by each ministry. In a third column list the number of people reached by those ministries who are not members of the church. Total the numbers in the second and third columns. You will find that if the number reached outside the church by your church's ministries is 15 percent or more, then your church is likely growing. These ministries don't have to be evangelistic in nature; they can be social outreach ministries as well.

— Thirteen —

Reflective Readings

O God, whose blessed Son did manifest himself to his disciples in the breaking of bread: Open, we pray thee, the eyes of our faith, that we may behold him in all his redeeming work; through the same thy Son Jesus Christ our Lord, who liveth and reigneth with thee, in the unity of the Holy Spirit, one God, now and for ever. Amen.

Reflective Readings are less content-filled than Teachings. They are designed not so much to give vestry members new information as they are to bring to the forefront of awareness what the vestry members likely already know from their own experience. Like Mental Exercises, these Reflective Readings should be used only occasionally. They will not cause vestry members to propose any immediate changes. Instead, they will simply heighten vestry members' awareness of issues that the congregation faces in intangible areas such as change, atmosphere, and momentum.

Reflective Reading 1
What Drives Your Church?

One of the most influential books currently read by pastors and lay leaders in America is *The Purpose-Driven Church,* by Rick Warren, pastor of one of the largest and most innovative churches in America. This book is must reading for all church leaders, whether lay or ordained, who wants to see their local church become more effective in its missional focus. Although not every church can use Warren's book as a blueprint for ordering its common life, the principles in the book are invaluable and beneficial to every church, regardless of its size.

Every church is driven by something. What drives your church? Tradition, finances, programs, personalities, events, seekers, and even buildings can be the controlling forces in a church. Some churches are maintenance-driven: success is simply getting the bills paid and keeping the doors open.

What is it that drives your church?

Once I bought copies of Warren's book for my vestry and had them read the chapter titled "What Is a Purpose-Driven Church?" Then I handed out index cards and asked them to fill in the blank: "Our church is a _____-driven church."

Then I read the responses, and they were what one would expect: We are a money-driven church, a tradition-driven church, a buildings-driven church, and so on. Each one had a good explanation for what had been written.

The very last one I read caught me by surprise and caught everyone else's attention as well. God used the last response to speak directly to the vestry. What were we?

We were a *crisis-driven* church.

When I read that card aloud, the word struck the heart of every vestry member. In our discussion that ensued, we knew that this one vestry member — a twenty-five-year member of the church, by the way — had spoken the truth.

The vestry acknowledged this truth about itself and set about getting out of the crisis mode that it had gotten stuck in. They began to focus on vision and policy rather than micromanaging and name-calling. They began to relate to each other in a less confrontational and more healthily relational way. And they began to recognize their own need to focus on the opportunities of the future rather than the problems of the past.

They began to put things together for their church so that the best years of the church would be in the future rather than in the past.

So what drives your church?

Is that what you believe God wants you to be driving your church?

If not, what are you going to do about it?

Questions for Reflection

• *Reflect on your last several vestry meetings. What did you spend the greatest amount of time discussing? finances? mission? new ministries? What does that tell you about what is deemed important?*

• *Pass out index cards to your vestry members and ask them to fill in the blank: "Our church is a _____-driven church." Discuss the results.*

Reflective Reading 2
The Crucible of Leadership

What makes a leader? My shorthand definition of leadership is that leaders solve problems with and through other people.

Warren Bennis and Robert Thomas wrote on this in the *Harvard Business Review.* They said that "one of the most reliable indicators and predictors of true leadership is an individual's ability to find meaning in negative events and to learn from even the most trying circumstances." They go on to say that "the skills required to conquer adversity and emerge stronger and more committed than ever are the same ones that make for extraordinary leaders."

In other words, life happens to everyone. All along our way we are tested by life's circumstances. Those who extract wisdom from both their failures as well as their successes emerge as leaders. Here's a story from my own experience:

The Young Priest and the Organist

The church organist had resigned two weeks earlier in protest over a decision I had made. Since then, several parishioners had come to me asking me to apologize to this beloved organist and rehire her. I had been at the church a little over a year. I was a young rector with a congregation of people considerably older than myself.

People asked, Wasn't I being a bit rash? Couldn't I give in a little bit because musicians are, as we know, a bit high strung? Didn't I realize that the church couldn't really handle this kind of conflict?

These conversations were all swirling in my thoughts as I was visiting with a former senior warden of the parish. He said, "You do realize that people are watching you, don't you? Many people, both inside the church and outside, are watching to see if you're going to cave in. There are a lot of people pulling for you."

Upon further investigation, I discovered that this organist had resigned under each of my two predecessors. Each rector had encountered conflict with this organist, who had resigned in protest each time until the rector relented.

When I shared this with my clergy support group, one of my fellow priests sent me *Antagonists in the Church,* by Richard Haugk, which showed me how to navigate these rapids with integrity. Those were lonely, lonely days and nights. At the end of this reading, I'll tell you "the rest of the story." However, the outcome was really less important for my learning and growth than the process. I later discovered that it was my character that was being formed.

Leaders Are Formed

While it is true that some people seem to have "natural leadership abilities," life is what actually forms leaders. A key component of leadership formation is character development. Robert Clinton in *The Making of a Leader* writes that God uses integrity checks to evaluate our intentions in order to test our character. He says that there are three parts to an integrity check:

1. the challenge to consistency with inner convictions;

2. the response to the challenge; and

3. the resulting expansion of ministry.

Recall the story of Daniel (Daniel 1:8–21) who faced an integrity check that could have cost him his life. Daniel and his three friends, not wanting to become ritually unclean, chose not to eat the food and drink offered by the king. God honored their faithfulness and blessed their obedience.

As emerging leaders we face a series of integrity checks all along the way. Often, however, we face early on a big integrity check that determines whether integrity is instilled in our character. Some do not pass integrity checks. King Saul in 1 Samuel 15 failed the integrity check in his life. As a result God gave the kingdom of Israel to another.

The good news is that our God is a God of second chances. Peter was tested numerous times. Nebuchadnezzar as well. The apostle Paul refused to take John Mark with him and Barnabas on a mission trip to Syria because John Mark had earlier abandoned them on a previous trip. In 2 Timothy 4:11, Paul admonishes Timothy to bring Mark with him because he was helpful to Paul in the ministry. In the Christian life, failure is never really final. But our ability to lead as well as the opportunities to grow in responsibility are often stymied by our failure to pass a key integrity test in our life.

An Exercise for Reflection

Reflect on your own life. Was there a time when you didn't pass an integrity check? Or when you did? Are there times when God brought circumstances your way that have lovingly confronted you with these same issues? As we are faithful in the small things, God will give us responsibility over larger things.

The Rest of the Story . . .

So what happened at that church? I did stand firm in my convictions, and we eventually hired a new organist. The truly important thing, though, was that the rector actually became the rector. Up until that time, it was the loudest voices that held sway in the congregation. As I learned to stand firm and with integrity, the church emerged stronger as it accepted the leadership of the rector.

It wasn't really about me or about whether I got my way. It was about right order and appropriate submission in the church. As I stood resolute — not alone but in conversation with those fellow leaders around me and with God — I grew, and the church grew as well.

Reflective Reading 3
How to Boil an Egg

My bishop is a non-anxious presence par excellence. The other day our bishop gathered the clergy of the diocese for a day of teaching, a Eucharist in which we reaffirmed our ordination vows and a time of conversation between the bishop and his clergy. When he was discussing a hot topic with a group of agitated people recently, I was struck — and not for the first time — with how calm he was. I have seen many times when people all around him are very animated and agitated while he appears calm and serene. When he gets involved in an emotion-filled discussion, it is as if he is in a zone of calm that often defuses the situation.

I asked him how he can be so calm so often in those emotion-filled exchanges. He said that it was because he learned years ago how to boil an egg.

How to Boil an Egg

So here's how to boil an egg and learn how to be calm in uncalm situations:

1. Place the egg in a saucepan.
2. Run cold water into the saucepan until the water is 1 inch above the egg.
3. Place the saucepan on the stove and cook over medium heat until the water begins to boil.
4. Reduce the heat to low.
5. Cook the egg until it reaches the desired consistency (2–3 minutes for soft-boiled and 10–15 for hard-boiled).

The point is that most of us non-cooks would place the egg in boiling water until it becomes hard-boiled. Keeping the heat at a boiling temperature will result in a cracked shell. Lowering the heat to low will cook the egg adequately without breaking the shell.

So often our conversations get heated too high; our emotions carry us away; we interrupt the other person because we feel like we *have* to get our point in; and we say things that we later wish we had not said. We listen to the other person just long enough to get our "word in edgewise," often interrupting because the other person just doesn't seem to get it. As the conversation gets hotter and hotter, the water boils longer and longer, and the shell of the egg ends up cracking.

Four Points to Remember

So how do we apply this lesson to emotion-filled situations?

First, know your foundational principles. This would be either the theology that guides you or the values that are non-negotiable. If you don't know what you're willing to surrender and why in a conflicted situation, you'll be willing to give in more in the "heat of the moment" than you are really comfortable with upon later reflection.

Second, find your own voice. Ask yourself, When you speak who is speaking? When we first become leaders, we read books, listen to tapes, and so on, as we learn others' vocabulary and ways of articulating things, gleaning from others' experience. Somewhere along the way something clicks into place: we become our own person as a leader. Instead of repeating others' words, we realize that the words we speak are our words, and the truth is affirmed from within us. We find our own voice as a leader. If you don't find your own voice, you will end up sounding like you're "reading someone else's mail." Your words will sound hollow and trite, without the ring of authenticity. Then, in a pinch, you will end up reverting to your emotional, inarticulate self because you haven't found the deeper person who is the real you.

Third, be comfortable with listening. If you are really listening to the other person, you will have less opportunity to say something you'll regret later. Proverbs 29:20 says, "Do you see someone who is hasty in speech? There is more hope for a fool than for anyone like that" (NRSV). View others as advisors rather than adversaries. Although you may not agree with them, really hearing them will help you respond in a non-defensive, non-threatening way. You might try arguing in your own mind from their perspective.

Fourth is a variation on the third, and that is, be comfortable with silence. In a heated discussion, no one is really going to convince anyone else. It is generally more important — and effective — for the other person to be heard than for you to get your "zinger" in.

Questions for Reflection

- *Think back on the last time you were involved in an emotion-filled conversation. Did you "turn the heat all the way up"? Or were you a calming influence? Which would you really rather be?*

- *Whom do you know that can calm a tension-filled situation? How does that person do it?*

- *Whom do you know that is good at exacerbating a tension-filled situation? How does that person do it?*

Reflective Reading 4
How to Reduce the Size of Your Congregation

I've never encountered a church that did not want to grow. Most of our churches would like to have more members, more involvement, more resources available for ministry. But let's face it, as a denomination, we are much better at reducing the size of our congregations than we are at growing them. Our Episcopal Church has lost over a million members—a third of our membership—since 1965.

Some of our churches are understandably less than enthusiastic about their future. For some, it seems that their past is more significant than their future. Several years ago Lyle Schaller, the "Father of Church Consultants," wrote an article on how to reduce the size of our congregations, on which the following is based.

1. ***Don't have a vision.*** Most parish profiles prepared for the search of a new rector will begin with the history of the congregation rather than the vision of the congregation. As Yogi Berra said, "If you don't know where you're going, you probably won't get there."

2. ***Encourage a low level of commitment by the members.*** Encourage the ratio of attendance-to-membership to be under 40 percent. Choose low-commitment people for key policymaking positions. ("Let's elect so-and-so to the vestry; maybe she will get more involved.")

3. ***Offer dull and boring worship services.*** Don't worry about whether visitors can follow the service. If they really want to be there, they'll get used to it.

4. ***Reduce the schedule during July and August.*** Encourage the church and Sunday school leaders to take an earned two-month vacation — at the time when people are moving into your community and looking for a church. This will encourage newcomers to look to those churches that offer a heavy program schedule for those months.

5. ***When people begin to demand choices, offer two: take it or leave it.*** "If you don't like how we do things here, go somewhere else."

6. ***Urge your pastor to adopt a highly non-directive or "laid back" leadership style.*** Let everyone do whatever they want to do. Casting lots worked in the call of Matthias, didn't it?

7. ***Allocate at least 60 percent of total expenditures for compensation of staff.*** Don't worry at all about offering programs for people to get involved in.

8. ***If you are crowded on Sunday morning (regularly 80 percent or more of the seats taken), don't add another service or build new facilities.*** That overcrowding problem will rectify itself eventually.

9. ***Don't get involved in foreign missions.*** Certainly, we have enough needs in our own neighborhood; we don't need to be sending our money or people overseas until we meet all our local needs.

10. ***Ignore first-time visitors, and don't even worry about incorporating them into the life of the congregation.*** Chances are that nobody helped you become a part of the congregation. If you can make it, they can, too.

Questions for Reflection

◆ *Reflect on why you want your church to grow. To have more people? To balance the budget? Because you think you're supposed to?*

◆ *Do you really want your church to grow? How small could your church get before people start getting upset? How much larger could your church get before people start getting upset?*

- *Does your congregation have more experience growing or shrinking in size? What factors have contributed to that growth or decline?*

- *Look around you. Find a church in circumstances similar to yours that has grown in the past thirty-five years. Ask them how they did it.*

Reflective Reading 5
In Praise of Passion

I recently had two experiences, both of which had a powerful impact on me. The first was at one of our Episcopal seminaries, where I was at a conference. We attended daily Eucharist in which faculty members celebrated each day. What caught my attention was how lacking in energy were the celebrants as they proclaimed the gospel through the liturgy. One celebrant in particular, rather than expressing a positive proclamation of the resurrection gave me the impression of how really sad it was that Jesus had died.

The other experience was at one of the churches in our diocese. After the sermon the preacher received a standing ovation. His sermon was passionate, Scripture-based, and full of illustrations from his life. He offered as a competent and informed exegesis of the text. It was both an intellectual as well as an emotional feast.

The Challenge of a Cool Spirituality

The typical formality of our liturgy has produced what Loren Mead describes in *Five Challenges for the Once and Future Church* as a "cool spirituality." He writes that what he learned about "growing into God was surrounded by *oughts:* how one ought to pray, how one cleansed oneself for communion with God." Mead felt that this way to God was a long and difficult road "with many detours — on which I seemed to be most of the time. There was not a lot of joy associated with the walk."

His response was to challenge the Episcopal Church to incorporate a more charismatic expression into its worship life. Mead compares and contrasts the traditional expressions of spirituality with a more charismatic spirituality. When the traditional form of spirituality decays, Mead says, it becomes lifeless: "Many members of the traditional churches have lived in such a straitjacket of their tradition that they have never found the power available in that very tradition — consequently their lives quietly go rigid and dry." Younger generations, he says, "unwilling to pack the emotions in dry ice, simply opt . . . for other venues in which to find vitality." He then compares a decaying traditional spirituality with a decaying charismatic spirituality. "When charismatic spirituality decays, it goes in another direction. As in the case of traditional spirituality, it becomes a parody of its strengths. Charismatic spirituality at its worst degenerates into spiritual pride" (pp. 30–39).

Mead thinks that our usual way of managing such differences is to choose one form over the other, to embrace one spirituality and eliminate the other. He suggests that the necessary solution is to view these polar opposites not as exclusive categories in which the church chooses one expression of spirituality and denigrates the other but rather to find creative ways for them to coexist. Polar opposites actually need each other to maintain health. The health of the church is enhanced by the vitality of each of these expressions of spirituality. Mead is calling essentially for the "warming up" of the spirituality temperature in Episcopal worship and the fostering of greater intimacy among the worshipers.

Warm Up the Worship through the Preacher's and Celebrant's Passion

The key to warming up our worship is not to go out and change the music right away, although that might help a little later. The key to warming up our worship is to develop more passion.

I used to post a note on the pulpit of the churches that I served that said, "What are you trying to get them to do, anyway?" This constantly reminded me that part of my role as preacher was to motivate people to action. Passion is an integral component of motivation.

Now, I'm not talking about ginning up a little emotionalism. That comes across about as well as a celebrant using a stained-glass voice. I am talking expressing a real and authentic passion that gives people a reason to believe, to trust, and to sacrifice.

How to Promote Passion

1. *Believe that passion is essential.* Søren Kirkegaard warned of the danger of the church losing its passion for the gospel and treating it instead like a "piece of information." Passion risks being replaced with descriptions of passion in other people.

2. *Pray for more passion.* You have to want passion to develop more passion within yourself. If you believe that passion is beneath you, all your attempts at expressing passion will come across as hollow. Do you believe that you can really make a difference in people's lives? Chances are, if you don't believe that, you will also lack passion.

3. *Get in touch with your passion.* What have you been passionate about before in your life? What are you passionate about now? The church in Ephesus was warned to return to its first love. Another way of approaching this is to reflect on why you entered into ministry in the first place. What has changed?

4. *Read the liturgy afresh.* When was the last time you read the liturgy in thankfulness for God's sacrifice and the forgiveness of your sins? The liturgy retells the great story of redemption. It tells not only my history but, praise God, my future. A sign on the dressing mirror of the sacristy of the church where I celebrate the Eucharist says, "Celebrate this mass, O priest of God, as if it were your first mass, your last mass, your only mass."

5. *Rate yourself on the passion meter.* Videotape or record a sermon or teaching or worship service (whatever the venue in which you lead). Where do you rate on a passion scale of one to ten? A former professor, who was Presbyterian, said that the national anthem of the Presbyterian Church should be, "Into my head, into my head, come into my head, Lord Jesus." What are you trying to get them to do, anyway? Why would your hearers want to respond to you? Or are you simply trying to get them to give a mental assent?

6. *Hang around passionate people.* How many people do you spend time with who remind you of Winnie the Pooh? As the storm

clouds gathered he nonchalantly remarked, "Tut, tut, it looks like rain"? Hang around people who recharge your batteries on a consistent basis, people who will fuel the fire of your soul.

Questions for Reflection

+ *Is there a difference between emotion and passion? What is it?*

+ *Reflect on a time when you were inspired to make a change in your life. What helped you in your resolve?*

+ *Who in your life inspires you to be better, work harder, and so on? Why? Is there someone in whose life you are making a difference? If so, why? If not, what might you do about it?*

Reflective Reading 6
The Changing Nature of Ministry

Returning to the Dallas area after an absence of thirty years has given me pause to reflect on the changes that have taken place both in terms of the Metroplex as well as ministry in the local church.

Thirty years ago the Cowboys were winning, the Rangers were rich in pitching and poor in batting, the Dallas Tornado was a great soccer team, and the semi-pro hockey team battled continually with the Fort Worth team (it was actually more dangerous in the stands than on the ice). Thirty years ago the Metroplex was not yet; the Dallas/Ft. Worth turnpike was still charging tolls; and Central Expressway was experimenting with the traffic lights to allow cars to enter onto the expressway—with two lanes in each direction.

Thirty years ago in the Episcopal Church, we did not yet realize that we were at the front end of a thirty-year decline in membership. Forty years earlier, in 1965, we were at the high point of our membership with 3.6 million members. Now we stand at 2.3 million members.

How has the face of ministry changed over these last thirty to forty years?

First, it is clear that pastoral ministry is much more complex than it was forty years ago. The makeup of family structures is much more complex than forty years ago. Blended families, single-parent families, singles, prolonged life spans have made ministering to families much more challenging.

Another example involves ministering to — and with — youth. The information and image revolution has changed the way we process information. As a society, we are much more visually oriented and less text-oriented than forty years ago. This is particularly true for our youth who grew up with the Internet, broadband, cell phones.

Another change is that the social pressure to attend church in the 1950s and early 1960s does not exist today. Back then, Christianity held "home court advantage." I remember praying the Lord's Prayer in public school and memorizing Psalms 23, 100, and 121 in class. We had the Sunday "Blue Laws," which outlawed the sale of certain goods on Sundays; now, most youth soccer tournaments in my part of the country play games on Sunday mornings.

Further, "Father Knows Best" was the prevailing attitude toward our clergy. Providing adequate pastoral care and good liturgy were enough to cause the average church to grow. Now, there is a much greater emphasis placed on the competence, personality, and performance of our clergy.

Another change involves the automobile. Lyle Schaller, a congregational consultant, says that he wishes that the one thing that our churches would accept is the reality that the automobile is here to stay. Many of our churches built before 1965 have woefully inadequate parking. Many of our churches operate as if it were the responsibility of city government to provide streets for parking for our churches. People don't mind driving past two or three Episcopal churches to find one that suits their needs, but they do want adequate parking.

These changes in our external culture bring great challenges to the church. A shoe salesman once went to a new territory in the mountains of Tennessee and left discouraged because nobody in that community wore shoes. A new salesman came along and wired to the main office, "I've hit a goldmine! Nobody wears shoes here! Send more samples!"

We serve a creative God who touches us within and through culture and whose truth is beyond all cultural changes. What an exciting time to be engaged in ministry!

Questions for Reflection

• *How has ministry in your church changed over the years?*

• *What parts of your church life are changeless?*

• *What parts of your church life change over time?*

• *What would you change about your church if you could?*

Reflective Reading 7
The Visitor Who Never Returned

Have you ever looked at your church through the eyes of a newcomer? You might make some interesting discoveries. Walk with me on an imaginary tour of a church by a first-time visitor (we'll call her Sue) as we explore what she might encounter or the questions she might ask. Sue is a thirty-two-year-old mom with two children, ages nine months and four years.

As she approaches your church, what does she see? An attractive building and well-manicured lawn? Or unkempt grass, growing weeds, unedged sidewalks?

What about the church sign? Is it lighted? Crisply painted? Accurate? What direction does it face? Can it be read easily by someone driving by the church at the posted speed? Signs that are parallel to the street can generally be read only by people walking by. How many people walk by your church to get information? Some churches put out acrylic tubes or holders with a leaflet describing the ministries of the church similar to what you'd see in front of houses for sale.

Where will she park? Do you have reserved parking for visitors and newcomers? Who gets the best parking places? The rector or vicar? The people who arrive earliest? You might consider having your staff and vestry or bishop's committee members park in the spots farthest away and save the best places for others.

By the way, how does your parking lot look? Is it clearly striped? Does it challenge the best shocks on a new car?

Do Sue and her children know where to go? Is it obvious where the sanctuary is? How will she find the nursery? What is the condition of the nursery? Would you put your baby or grandbaby in that nursery? Are the toys old? When were the toys last sanitized? How about the sheets in the cribs? Diapers? Wipes? Some churches instruct their childcare workers to change every baby's diaper fifteen minutes before the worship service will end — even if the diaper doesn't need changing. This assures that the mother will get her baby back with a fresh diaper. Is there a sign-in sheet? What will prevent someone from off the street coming to get Sue's baby pretending to be the father or aunt? What year does your nursery look like — 2007 or 1955?

Are there clear signs pointing Sue to where she needs to go? Many visitors don't really want to ask directions (men are particularly fond of finding their way without asking for help). Are the restrooms clearly marked? Are they clean? How do they compare with the restrooms at Wal-Mart or McDonald's?

Sue finally gets to the worship service. How are the ushers? Warm and friendly or "officious"? Are they seating people for a funeral or to celebrate the resurrection of Jesus Christ? Do they proactively help to seat Sue, or do they view their job as finished once they've handed her the bulletin?

Once Sue sits down, will she find it easy to follow the service? Or will she have to learn the "Episcopal shuffle": Pick up the bulletin, pick up the prayer book, put down the prayer book, look up the hymn number, pick up the hymnal, put down the hymnal, look up the page number in the Book of Common Prayer (what's that?), oops, no, we're in the Bible now. It's on the leaflet? I have four different leaflets. Oops, everyone's kneeling and I'm still standing. Oh, I'm so embarrassed. Now, I'm kneeling and everyone else is sitting.

Does Sue get personally invited to Coffee Hour? Where is it? Can it compete with Starbucks? Will anybody talk to her, or will she stand there and watch people being very friendly to each other but not to her?

Do not neglect to show hospitality to strangers, for by doing that some have entertained angels without knowing it.

(Heb 13:2, NRSV)

Questions for Reflection

• *If Sue were to visit your church, what would her experience be?*

• *As a group, talk through what Sue experienced in this story with what she might experience at your church.*

Fourteen

The Vestry Selection Process

Here are some sample guidelines from a church that we will call St. Alban's.

A. Vestry Election Guidelines

The vestry is a body of non-ordained persons in the Episcopal Church, duly elected by the members of the church to provide oversight with the rector of the spiritual and material concerns of the parish. The vestry specifically authorizes all financial obligations of the church and oversees the church properties.

In accordance with the canons of the Diocese of Strategery, the Vestry shall consist of nine to eighteen persons, each of whom shall be elected for a term of three years. Our current vestry consists of nine persons. Persons who have served a three-year term or a two-year term to complete an unexpired term are ineligible to serve for a period of one year. Vestry members who have served to complete a one-year unexpired term are eligible to serve a full three-year term.

The Nomination and Election Process

A nominating committee will serve to receive and to make nominations to the vestry. The committee will consist of the senior warden as chair, the outgoing members of the vestry not eligible for election, and the rector as pastoral consultant. The committee will meet following the September vestry meeting. Recommendations will be solicited from the congregation at large in the September newsletter. The committee will meet on October 9, 2007, with those persons who have been recommended. During the following week, these persons will fast and pray concerning whether God is calling them to serve on the vestry. Those who feel led will be nominated, and information on the nominees will be published in the November newsletter. The election for new vestry members will be held on the first Sunday in December during the Sunday school hour.

Nominations must be in writing using the form provided by the church and turned in to the church office by Friday, October 7, 2007. The person being nominated must have given approval for his or her name to be put in nomination.

Canonical Requirements

Confirmed Communicant in Good Standing of St. Alban's Church, at least eighteen years of age.

Spiritual Requirements

1. To have a commitment to Jesus Christ as Lord and Savior and to subscribe to the vision statement of St. Alban's Church.

2. To have been active in the life and ministry of the St. Alban's Church for one year.

3. To commit to spiritual growth, with a discipline of Bible study and prayer. One evidence of this commitment is that the person attends, teaches, or leads a small group or Sunday school class.

4. To be a faithful steward and committed to proportional giving, with the tithe as the goal.

5. To have family relationships that reflect strong Christian commitment and support the person being a vestry member.

B. Vestry Candidate Recommendations

I wish to recommend _____ to serve on the Vestry of St. Alban's Church.

I believe that God is calling this person to serve on the Vestry for the following reasons:

I understand that this person and the nominating committee will enter a period of discernment to seek God's will in this matter. I agree to support this process by my prayers.

Signature of person making the recommendation:

_____

I have read the requirements to serve on the vestry and affirm them, and consent to to my being nominated.

Signature of person being recommended, designating consent to be nominated, and willingness to serve if elected:

_____

Requirements

1. To have a commitment to Jesus Christ as Lord and Savior and to subscribe to the vision statement of St. Alban's Church.

2. To have been active in the life and ministry of St. Alban's Church for one year.

3. To commit to spiritual growth, with a discipline of Bible study and prayer. One evidence of this commitment is that the person attends, teaches, or leads a small group or Sunday school class.

4. To be a faithful steward and committed to proportional giving, with the tithe as a goal.

5. To have family relationships that reflect strong Christian commitment and support the person being a Vestry member.

Vestry membership should not be considered an honor for past service but rather a commitment to future service.

C. Sample Commissioning Rite for Vestry Members

Celebrant   Brothers and Sisters in Christ Jesus, we are all baptized by the one Spirit into one Body, and given gifts for a variety of ministries for the common good. Our purpose is to commission these persons in the Name of God and of this congregation to a special ministry to which they are called. These persons are prepared by a commitment to Jesus Christ as Lord, by regular attendance at worship, and by knowledge of their duties, to exercise their ministry to the honor of God and the well-being of his church.

Celebrant   You have been called to the ministry of serving on the vestry in this congregation. Will you, as long as you are engaged in this work, perform it with diligence?

Candidates   I will.

Celebrant   Will you be faithful in your prayer life and your stewardship of your time and resources, and will you seek the will of Christ for his church above your own?

Candidates   I will.

Celebrant   Will you faithfully and reverently execute the duties of your ministry to the honor of God and the benefit of this congregation?

Candidates   I will.

Celebrant   Hear the Word of the Lord from Numbers, chapter 11, verses 16 and 17: "The Lord said to Moses: 'Bring me seventy of Israel's elders who are known to you as leaders and officials among the people. Have them come to the Tent of Meeting, that they may stand there with you.' 'I will come down and speak with you there, and I will take of the Spirit that is on you and put the Spirit on them. They will help you carry the burden of the people so that you will not have to carry it alone.'"

Let us pray.

O God, our Supreme Leader, give your blessing and guidance to these your servants commissioned to serve as vestry members in your church, that by word and example they may serve those whom they lead and exemplify your care for us; and may they seek the mind of Christ in his will for this church through Jesus Christ our Lord. *Amen.*

In the Name of God and this congregation, I commission you, the Vestry Members, in this congregation for the year _____ .